Using Literature to Teach Middle Grades about War

Phyllis K. Kennemer

ORYX PRESS
1993

The rare Arabian Oryx is believed to have inspired the myth of the unicorn. This desert antelope became virtually extinct in the early 1960s. At that time several groups of international conservationists arranged to have 9 animals sent to the Phoenix Zoo to be the nucleus of a captive breeding herd. Today the Oryx population is nearly 800, and over 400 have been returned to reserves in the Middle East.

Copyright © 1993 by Phyllis K. Kennemer
Published by The Oryx Press
4041 North Central at Indian School Road
Phoenix, Arizona 85012-3397

Published simultaneously in Canada

Printed and Bound in the United States of America

∞ The paper used in this publication meets the minimum requirements of American National Standard for Information Science—Permanence of Paper for Printed Library Materials, ANSI Z39.48, 1984.

Library of Congress Cataloging-in-Publication Data

Kennemer, Phyllis K.
    Using literature to teach middle grades about war / by Phyllis K. Kennemer.
        p. cm.
    Includes bibliographical references and index.
    ISBN 0-89774-778-X
    1. Military history, Modern—Study and teaching (Secondary)—United States.   2. War—Study and teaching (Secondary)—United States.   3. Children's literature—Study and teaching (Secondary)—United States.   4. Interdisciplinary approach in education.
I. Title.
D214.K46   1992
940'.7'071273—dc20   92-31932
                                                                    CIP

*This book is lovingly dedicated
to my husband, Bob,
"the wind beneath my wings"*

Contents

Acknowledgments

Working with students as a classroom teacher, language arts teacher, and library media specialist for over 20 years has convinced me of the value of using thematic literature units to make learning more meaningful. Such units offer opportunities for all students to participate at their own levels of ability and interest.

During the last ten years I have conducted numerous sessions about planning and teaching literature units at local, state, and regional professional conferences. Many people have told me they adapted my suggestions and bibliographies into successful units. They often follow their remarks with, You really ought to write a book. Well, here is a book! I hope it will prove to be as helpful to teachers and librarians as was anticipated by those who requested it.

Writing a book turned out to be much more complicated and time-consuming than I expected. I attempted to find every book I could about wars that involved the United States. Reading all of the books was at times exhilarating, at times depressing, but always interesting.

I also discovered that writing a book is impossible without the support and help of friends and family. I would like to acknowledge some of these people.

Ronald Jobe of the University of British Columbia offered continuing encouragement and sent me information to help find appropriate books. Michael Tunnell and Carl Tomlinson of Northern Illinois University provided me some of their research and writings on the value of using trade books for teaching history, which helped to support my basic premise for writing the book.

Judy Volc of Boulder Public Library and Beth Elder of Denver Public Library aided me in finding numerous books. Bobbie Ponis, Coordinator of Library Media Services for Jefferson County School District in Colorado, gave me access to new books that came into her office. Library media specialists throughout the school district were on the alert for appropriate books and either called them to my attention or sent me copies from their own collections. The greatest help in this respect came from Marlene Lind of Kendallvue Elementary School in Littleton, Colorado.

Laurie Brock, my editor, offered encouragement when I needed it most and kept extending my deadlines to keep the book's completion a possibility.

My mother graciously invited Michelle, my 13-year-old, to spend two weeks with her this summer, providing me with the uninterrupted time needed to finish writing. There were many days during this past year when Michelle was called upon to exhibit more patience than is expected for her age, and she legitimately wondered if that book was ever going to be finished!

It is no exaggeration to say this book would not be possible without the constant loving support of my husband, Bob. He freed me up to read and write by taking care of many mundane tasks of everyday life. He was also my chief consultant and critic. His experiences as a history major in college and his lifelong interest in the wars proved very beneficial as we discussed numerous issues. His constructive comments on a continuous stream of rough drafts contributed immensely to the final product.

—Phyllis Kennemer

Introduction

The excitement and enjoyment of learning is increased through the use of literature-based units. Studying historical periods through literature offers an invigorating, interesting way to become immersed in a past era and thus gain a substantial understanding of the people involved, their conditions, and their decisions. Reading books that depict a wide range of viewpoints enables students to reach intelligent conclusions and to expand their learning through developing informed inquiries.

Thematic literature units provide a basis for meaningful learning experiences, encourage students to share the responsibility for their own learning, enhance the quality of individual student participation, and increase opportunities for using high-level thinking processes.

Basis for Meaningful Learning Experiences

The integration of history and literature provides a cogent combination for merging facts and feelings about a previous time period. The study of history comes alive when students think about an era in terms of the people who lived (or did not live) through it. Considering the people in terms of their life-styles, their circumstances for making decisions, and their dreams and aspirations helps young people become intellectually and emotionally involved. The study of wars has a powerful potential for engaging students' attention because lives and nations often change so drastically.

Students Share the Responsibility for Their Own Learning

Thematic literature units offer students many opportunities to make choices about their own learning. From lists of recommended books they may choose volumes appropriate to their reading abilities. They will then be prepared to make meaningful contributions during small and large group discussions. Their choices of activities and projects for presentation may reflect their particular talents, and they can make unique contributions to others' understanding. They share significant knowledge with classmates who would not, in many cases, acquire information about that particular topic in any other way.

Providing for Individual Differences

Although all students are reading books based on the same theme, they are not all reading the same books. Students with superior reading ability may choose to read longer, more complex books, while other students may select shorter, simpler materials.

The choice of projects can also be influenced by individual strengths and talents. Academically talented students may choose projects that require detailed research and extensive presentations. Students with artistic abilities may decide to do murals or posters, while students with speaking abilities may opt to participate in interviews or debates. Offering a wide variety of choices enables all students to make significant contributions.

Opportunities for Using High-Level Thinking Processes

Thematic literature units offer opportunities to explore complex issues from a variety of viewpoints. The issues involved in wars are often controversial, both during the time in which they occurred and in later analyses made by historians. Looking at the wars from a number of different perspectives challenges critical and creative thinking. If students have a good grasp of the events and prevalent thinking of the time, they can begin to ask their own questions about decisions that were made. What if . . . ? is one of the most effective beginnings for stimulating creative thought. After looking at a war in its historical context, exploring its influence on the world today offers additional opportunities for critical thinking. Students can begin to formulate their own questions and look for their own answers.

Wars Included in This Book

The wars included in this book are the Revolutionary War, the Civil War, World War I, World War II, the Vietnam War, and the Gulf War. The selection of these wars was based mainly on the availability of appropriate materials for young people. Wars that were considered, but eliminated due to limited materials, were the French and Indian War, the War of 1812, the Mexican-American War, and the Korean War.

A unit on the Gulf War is included because of the intense interest in this recent conflict. Even though materials on the Gulf War are still limited, it is likely that many factual books and biographies will be available. (Fiction books and picture books traditionally appear some years after the conclusion of a war.) The unit included for this war can provide a framework for planning a meaningful course of study using articles in magazines and newspapers. Appropriate books may be added as they become available.

Using This Resource Book

Using Literature to Teach Middle Grades about War provides teachers and school librarians with a basic framework for designing thematic units. A wide variety of resources for use in planning and teaching literature units is included. The resources and units are recommended for use with students in grades 6 through 8, although the units could easily be adapted for higher or lower grade levels.

Educators are welcome to use any component in this book as it is written, but most instructors will prefer to adapt, not adopt, these components as they design lesson plans based on their objectives for the study and the needs of their students.

Cooperative Planning

Although these units can be planned and taught by individual teachers, it is desirable to involve other knowledgeable educators whenever possible. If the school has a qualified librarian who is also a certified teacher, the librarian can be a valuable team member throughout the unit. Teachers and librarians may collaborate on unit objectives, designate the skills to be taught, and decide on books and other resources needed. The librarian can then participate by teaching research skills, assisting students, leading group discussions, locating resources within the school, and borrowing resources from other schools and libraries. References to teachers throughout this book apply equally well to qualified school librarians. (See appendix A for a planning guide for teachers and librarians.)

In some schools it may be possible for the librarian to take responsibility for a small, special interest group in the library for several weeks. (See appendix A for a planning guide for special interest groups.)

Cooperative planning and teaching may also take place among teachers of various disciplines. A history or social studies teacher can team up with a language arts teacher, for instance. Whatever the combination, include the school librarian whenever possible.

Grouping for Thematic Units

Large Groups

Thematic literature units work well for entire classes, providing opportunities to accommodate a wide range of learning styles, abilities, and talents. Suggested teaching plans for total classes are provided as a component of each unit.

Small Groups

Sometimes it is desirable to establish special interest groups. These are groups of students who choose to study a particular theme for a specified period of time (generally varying from two to six weeks). Such groups should usually be limited to ten or fewer students who have demonstrated the ability to work independently. They meet with the teacher or librarian for an introduction to the unit and to discuss guidelines, and then do much of the reading and activities on their own. Periodic meetings led by the teacher or librarian provide them with opportunities to share the books they have been reading and to present projects they have prepared. Students are required to read a specified minimum number of books from each category and fill out a reporting form for each book read. More books than the minimum requirement may be read for extra credit. Grades can then be based on the number of books or the number of pages read and the quality of project presentations. (See appendix B for book reporting forms and a group record keeping form.)

Components of Each Unit

All of the units in this resource guide have the basic components described below.

Selected Chronology

Each chronology provides a quick overview of the war's major events, helping to place these events in historical perspective. Underlying causes for wars often brew for many years, so significant events that took place long before the war are sometimes noted. No attempt was made to include all of the battles fought in any war. The first and major battles are included to show the scope of the war or to note turning points for the eventual outcome. Battles that are the subject of or serve as background for one of the recommended readings are also included. Most dates are general, listing the year and month to provide an overall time frame for thinking about the war. Specific dates are included when significant. The Selected Chronology can be duplicated and used as a quick reference for teachers and students.

Recommended Books

An effort was made to locate and read as many books as possible relating to the six wars. Books were selected for inclusion based on the appropriate evaluative criteria for each genre, with attention to readability, copyright dates, and point of view. Most of the books are appropriate for students in grades 6 through 8. A few books were included for more mature readers, and some high-quality, easy-to-read books were included to enable reluctant readers to contribute to discussions. All such books are noted in the annotations. Number of pages is a good indicator of reading difficulty: Shorter books are generally easier reading; longer books are more difficult.

The annotations give concise book summaries and provide some indication of the tone of the writing. Because presenting a variety of viewpoints was one of the objectives, annotations attempt to provide a clear description of each book's point of view.

An attempt was made to find books with recent copyright dates, partly because they are more likely to still be in print. Older books are included when they are classics in the field or when nothing of a later copyright could be found on a specific subject or with a particular point of view. Publishing information is given for hardback editions, unless paperback is specified in the bibliographic information. Many of the recommended titles are available in paperback and may be purchased in multiple copies. A few suggestions for such purchases are recommended in the Sample Lesson Plan sections in some units.

The information provided for each book includes series title (if any), author, type of illustration and name of illustrator, publisher, publication date, number of pages, and inclusion of special sections, such as bibliography, index, chronology, etc.

Books other than the ones recommended may, of course, be included in literature units about these wars. Teachers and librarians are encouraged to search for additional books and materials and evaluate them based on literary criteria and the unit's objectives.

Each unit has recommendations for picture books, factual books, biographies, and fiction books. These classifications are arranged in the order they are used in the Sample Lesson Plans. Each classification serves a special purpose within the literature unit; combining all of these types of books helps students gain a balanced perspective of the war.

Picture Books

Carefully selected picture books provide a common experience for all students at the beginning of a unit and at several points within the unit. These books usually take about 15 minutes to read aloud, allowing ample time within most class sessions for discussion of the issues presented and for additional sharing of information and questions about the war.

Factual Books

Most of these books are well researched, well written, and attractively formatted. They are generally written in a narrative style that engages the reader's interest. Some of these books present a broad overview of the war, while others focus on one event or aspect. Teachers and librarians may choose to supplement this section with textbooks, encyclopedias, and other reference materials available in school and public libraries.

Biographies

Reading biographies and autobiographies breathes life into historical studies. These books present portraits of leaders as real people with strengths and weaknesses who made decisions based on their personality traits and their understanding of the issues of the time. In retrospect, some of these decisions may have been in error, but it is necessary to grasp the context of the historical situation prior to questioning them.

Biographies of common soldiers and civilians are also included. These books provide a sense of the effects of war on all people.

Fiction Books

Most of the recommended historical fiction books are based on real people or actual events. Reading these books can provide a realistic sense of having lived during the time of the war through evoking some of the emotions and experiences of people of the time. Fiction books are especially valuable for providing wide ranges of viewpoints. Individual books present perspectives of the effects of war that are seldom found in textbooks or encyclopedias.

Sample Lesson Plans

The sample lesson plans were designed to encourage students to take some responsibility for their own learning. After sharing a common experience based on an appropriate picture book about the war, they are asked to share their knowledge of the subject and formulate their own questions. Students are encouraged to search for information in the school library and in classroom resources, which may include textbooks. They share their findings with others and move forward in building a knowledge base about the war. Although there are some suggestions for required readings and activities, students are given many opportunities for choice. They may select factual books that present major events in an easy-to-read style, or they may choose more complex books that offer a greater depth of understanding.

Students are encouraged to make meaningful contributions to their own and their classmates' knowledge through choosing projects for class presentations. Projects may be selected based on individual interests, talents, and skills. Suggestions for a wide variety of possible activities are included.

Lesson plans are based on the assumption that teachers and librarians are working together in planning and teaching the units. Students may, therefore, be moving back and forth between the classroom and the library throughout the units.

Suggested Questions

The suggested questions are intended to stimulate logical, critical, and creative thinking. Most of the questions are open-ended, addressing broad, significant issues. None can be answered with a simple yes or no. Opportunities are provided for using higher levels of thinking, including application, analysis, synthesis, and evaluation. Teachers are urged to keep in mind that students should not be asked to use these higher levels of thinking without a firm basis in knowledge and comprehension. Use of the suggested questions will generally be appropriate after the students have had some experience in reading about the wars and talking about what they've read.

Suggested Activities

The suggested activities offer students opportunities to become experts on a specific topic related to the war. Emphasis should be on doing careful research and designing presentations that provide other students with a meaningful understanding of the topic. An attempt was made to suggest projects that could be accomplished within reasonable time and resource limits, but that would also readily engage the students' attention—something they would not think of on their own. Some of the suggested activities are appropriate to challenge academically gifted students. They may choose to do in-depth studies within the classroom setting, as part of a special interest group, or as an independent study. All of the suggestions may be used to spark ideas for further activities as teachers and librarians consider their goals for the unit and the talents of the particular group of students.

Glossaries

The glossaries define words students may need to know as they read and study about the wars. The glossaries may be used for teacher and librarian referral when activities and discussions are planned, or they may be duplicated and given to students early in the unit. A few words can be selected for students to define using reference books, if this is an appropriate skill for the goals of the unit. Using the entire list for this purpose, however, is discouraged because it could dampen enthusiasm for further study.

Evaluations

Student evaluation in an entire class setting may be based on grades given throughout the unit for book reporting forms, projects, and participation in group discussions.

Evaluation for students in special interest groups can be based on similar criteria or on the total number of pages read during the unit, provided reporting forms and participation have been of high quality.

An overall evaluation of the unit by students for teacher use in future planning is highly recommended. Feedback from students is valuable in reenforcing the use of effective activities and making appropriate changes in others. (See appendix B for samples of evaluation, record keeping, and reporting forms.)

Appendixes

Appendix A contains planning guides for use by teachers and/or librarians as they design their instructional units. The first one provides suggested guidelines and questions to consider in advance as an aid in effectively organizing the units for classes or groups of classes. The second planning guide provides help in designing units for special interest groups.

Appendix B is composed of sample record keeping and reporting forms. Reporting forms for factual books, biographies, and fiction books are provided. These appear as one-page forms, but spacing may be expanded to provide for more informative responses. Also included is a record keeping form for tracking student progress and assisting in grading. An evaluation form for students to provide feedback about the unit concludes the section.

General Activities for Use with All Units

Involving students in activities and the creation of projects enables them to take some responsibility for their own learning and provides opportunities for them to share their knowledge with others.

The following activities can be used with any of the units included in this resource book. Activities appropriate to specific wars are included within each unit.

Small Group Discussions

Groups of four to six students provide all students with opportunities to participate in discussions. Students can be taught to be effective discussion leaders, recorders, and participants.

Guidelines for Discussion Leaders

1. Arrange chairs or desks so all group participants can see each other.
2. Base discussion on questions and issues that have been agreed upon. These may be determined by a meeting of the group leaders or may be distributed by the teacher at the beginning of the discussion period.
3. Try to include all group members in the discussion. Do not let one person dominate; ask for contributions from those who are not saying anything.
4. Summarize or paraphrase what people are saying, especially if the meaning is not immediately clear.
5. Be aware of time restrictions and keep the discussion moving so all relevant topics may be explored.

Guidelines for Group Recorders

1. Note down the names of people in the group.
2. Accurately record the essence of what is being said. Notes do not need to be recorded in full sentences. Jot down the main ideas as students are talking.
3. Ask for clarification of statements that are not clear.
4. Write the group's major conclusions on transparencies or chart paper to share with the rest of the class members.

Large Group Discussions

These discussions will usually be led by the classroom teacher or the school librarian, who may choose to have each group recorder share two or three major points from their small group discussions and then throw it open for general discussion by the class. Ten or fifteen minutes should be sufficient for summarizing and sharing after small group discussions.

Timelines

Timelines provide a clear method of keeping track of important dates and events throughout the study. Consider placing the names of people from biographies and characters from fiction books on the timeline, as well as dates of major battles.

Diaries or Journals

Entries can be made for a specific period (usually about one or two weeks) that could have been recorded in a diary or journal by a person living during the historical period being studied. Choices of people may include common soldiers or civilians as well as famous decision makers.

Debates

Many of the issues in these wars were, and some remain, controversial. Preparing for and participating in debates provides opportunities to study an issue in depth and share research with classmates in a meaningful way.

Interviews

Enacting television or radio interviews with historic people or book characters can provide an informative and entertaining way of presenting information.

Greet the Greats

For this activity, each student chooses one historical person or book character to impersonate. The student prepares to act as that individual for a school assembly or evening parent program, dressing as the chosen person and staying in character throughout the assembly or evening. Students may prepare displays about the people they are impersonating and stand with those displays while guests mingle about informally and ask questions, or a formal presentation can be held in which the impersonated individuals are interviewed about their participation in the war and their personal experiences. (See the Sample Lesson Plan for the Revolutionary War for instructions on the Return to the Revolutionary Era Event, which is based on this idea.)

Dramatic Presentations

Role playing is one method of exhibiting that important information has been internalized. Writing a script and presenting a play is a more formal way of demonstrating a summary of acquired knowledge and understanding.

Media Interpretations

Students may create a variety of media productions to demonstrate their understanding of concepts and people. Emphasis should be on communicating information to classmates in a meaningful manner. Types of media may include videotapes, computer programs, posters, charts, filmstrips, slide and audiotape shows, puppet shows, dioramas, and sets of transparencies.

Displays

Gathering memorabilia from the war being studied helps students comprehend the reality of the war. Students may make their own items for display as well. These may be simple drawings and cutouts made from paper and cardboard or more elaborate models of significant items.

Guest Speakers

Veterans or relatives of veterans of recent wars are sometimes willing to talk with students about their experiences. Scholars of the wars can be contacted at local universities. Be on the lookout for war buffs in your area. Often a local person has a strong interest in a specific war and has acquired knowledge and memorabilia that are worth sharing with students.

Field Trips

Excursions to local museums or historic sites can enhance the study of a historical period and help make the study more relevant to students.

Webbing Technique for Notetaking

Creating a series of webs for recording pertinent information is an effective way to take notes. Main topics for a subject may be assigned in advance or determined in the process of research. Each topic is written in the middle of a piece of plain paper. As details and supporting facts are found, they are written on lines extending out from the central topic. An outline of the subject can then be constructed from the webs.

Audiovisual Materials

Recommendations for audiovisual materials are not included in the scope of this resource book. Recordings, videotapes, and CD-ROM programs are available commercially and through libraries. Using these materials can add interest and understanding.

Using
Literature
to Teach
Middle Grades
about War

Revolutionary War Literature Unit

Selected Chronology

1763		End of the French and Indian War.
		The British decided to keep a standing army in North America.
		Proclamation of 1763 issued by Parliament.
1764		Sugar Act passed by Parliament.
1765		Quartering Act and Stamp Act passed by Parliament.
		Meeting of the Stamp Act Congress in New York.
1766		Parliament repealed the Stamp Act.
		The Declaratory Act passed by Parliament.
1767		Townshend Acts passed by Parliament.
1770	March 5	Boston Massacre.
		Parliament repealed the Townshend duties, except for the tax on tea.
1773	December 16	Boston Tea Party.
1774		Intolerable Acts passed by Parliament.
		First Continental Congress held in Philadelphia.
1775		Restraining Act passed by Parliament.
		Second Continental Congress held at Philadelphia.
	April 18	Paul Revere and William Dawes rouse the minutemen.
	April 19	First shot of the war fired near Lexington and Concord.
	May 10	Fort Ticonderoga taken by the companies of Ethan Allan and Benedict Arnold.
	June 17	Battle of Bunker Hill.
		Decision of the Second Continental Congress to establish an army.
	July 2	George Washington became the commander in chief of the Continental army.
	November/ December	American forces failed to seize Quebec and the conquest of Canada was abandoned.

1776	March	Henry Knox reached Boston with the cannon from Fort Ticonderoga.
	July 4	The Declaration of Independence was proclaimed by the Second Continental Congress.
	August	The British gained control of New York.
	December 25	General Washington defeated Colonel Johann Rull at Trenton.
1777	January 3	Washington won a victory at Princeton.
	July	General Burgoyne recaptured Ticonderoga.
	August	Benedict Arnold defeated Colonel Barry St. Leger.
	August	American General John Stark defeated a troop of Hessians at Bennington in Vermont.
	September	First Battle of Freeman's Farm.
	October	Second Battle of Freeman's Farm.
		General Burgoyne surrendered at Saratoga.
		France entered the war as an American ally.
	November 15	Congress adopted the Articles of Confederation.
	Winter	Washington's army camped at Valley Forge, Pennsylvania.
1778	June	Last major battle in the North fought at Monmouth, New York.
	December	A mixed force of British, Hessian, and Loyalist troops captured Savannah, Georgia.
	December	George Rogers Clark and a force of pioneers destroyed British centers along the frontier.
1779	July	General Anthony Wayne regained Stony Point for the Americans.
	September	John Paul Jones, Captain of the *Bonhomme Richard*, engaged in a battle at sea with the British navy.
1780		Failure of Benedict Arnold's plot to turn West Point over to the British.
	May 12	General Henry Clinton attained victory at Charleston.
	August 16	General Charles Cornwallis defeated General Horatio Gates' attempt to attack Camden, South Carolina.
1781	January 17	American Brigadier General Daniel Morgan defeated the British at Cowpens, South Carolina.
	October 19	Cornwallis surrendered at Yorktown.
	December	American Colonel Marinus Willett defeated frontier forces at Jerseyfield, New York.
1782	April	Peace talks began in Paris.
1783	September 3	Peace treaty signed.

Recommended Books

Picture Books

Boston Tea Party: Rebellion in the Colonies

(Adventures in Colonial America Series)
Written by James E. Knight
Illustrated by David Wenzel
Troll Associates, 1982
32 pages

Written in letter format dated 18 June 1774, this is a view of the Boston Tea Party as it might have been experienced by Benjamin Hatcher, a member of the Committee of Correspondence of Massachusetts. The letter is addressed to William Yancy, a member of South Carolina's Committee of Correspondence. The Boston Tea Party, the events leading up to the event, and the consequences are all related in a conversational tone.

Leonard Everett Fisher's Liberty Book

Compiled and illustrated by Leonard Everett Fisher
Doubleday & Company, 1976
48 pages

A collection of patriotic poems, songs, quotations, and pictures celebrate liberty. Bold illustrations in red, white, and blue dominate most pages in this oversize book. Notes about the sources of the selections are included.

Paul Revere's Ride

Written by Henry Wadsworth Longfellow
Illustrated by Ted Rand
Dutton Children's Books, 1990
40 pages

Dramatically illustrated in full color, this version brings Longfellow's famous poem to life. Beautifully detailed paintings capture the sense of intrigue and adventure of the moonlight ride to warn the colonists of the British attack in April 1775. Maps on the endpapers show the rides of Revere, Dawes, and Prescott on that fateful night.

Picture Book of Revolutionary War Heroes
Written and illustrated by Leonard Everett Fisher
Stackpole Books, 1970
62 pages

Fifty well-known and lesser-known people of the Revolutionary War period are presented on one-page spreads. Half of each page contains an illustration of the person in dark blue chiaroscuro, with the rest of the page devoted to a brief summary of the person's important role in the war effort. Fifteen representatives of each region—the New England Colonies, the Middle Colonies, and the Southern Colonies—and five foreign allies are included in this oversize book.

Pop! Goes the Weasel and Yankee Doodle
Written and illustrated by Robert Quackenbush
J. B. Lippincott, 1976
32 pages

Two favorite songs from the Revolutionary period are featured in contrasting historical and contemporary New York City settings. The historical illustrations are based on original paintings in the Museum of the City of New York and the New York Public Library. Modern views of New York were painted on location. The music for the songs and an illustrated tour of 18 historical sites in Manhattan are included.

Samuel's Choice
Written by Richard Berleth
Illustrated by James Watling
Albert Whitman & Company, 1990
[40 pages], map

This story of a teenaged slave who chose to help the Patriots is set against the background of General Washington's retreat from Brooklyn in 1776. First Samuel rows some of the Patriots across the river in his master's boat, and later during a violent storm he sets a line that enables Washington's troops to find their way across the water in the dark. Samuel is a slave who gained his freedom when his master was arrested and had his property confiscated for aiding the British.

Factual Books

The American Revolution
(American History Topic Books Series)
Written by Richard B. Morris
Illustrated by Leonard Everett Fisher
Lerner Publications Company, 1985
66 pages, index

A summary of the major events of the war covering the period from 2 July 1776, when the vote for independence was taken, through the signing of the Treaty of Paris in 1783. Major battles and important people are briefly described. The author includes sections connecting the significance of the war with implications for present times.

The American Revolutionaries:
A History in Their Own Words 1750–1800
Written by Milton Meltzer
Illustrated with black-and-white photographs
Thomas Y. Crowell, 1987
210 pages, bibliography, index

An anecdotal record of events featuring quotations from letters, diaries, and other personal documents. The beginning entries describe the settlement of the colonies and the deplorable conditions of life for many people of the time, including indentured servants and slaves. Selections about major events of the war and the participation of various groups, such as blacks and Indians, are included. The conflict between the Patriots and Loyalists is highlighted. Some of the entries were written by well-known individuals such as George Washington, Abigail Adams, and Benjamin Franklin. Other selections reveal the thoughts and experiences of the common people.

The Battle of Lexington and Concord
Written by Neil Johnson
Illustrated with color photographs
Four Winds Press, 1992
40 pages, bibliography

Photographs from the reenactment of these opening battles of the Revolutionary War bring this conflict to life. The well-written text examines the causes of colonist unrest, describes the battle in detail, and summarizes the results.

Black Heroes of the American Revolution

Written by Burke Davis
Illustrated with prints and portraits of the period
Harcourt Brace Jovanovich, 1976
80 pages, bibliography, index

The contributions of blacks during the war are recognized. Unfortunately, most of their names have been lost, but the people who are known serve as representatives of the many who served. Crispus Attucks, an escaped slave, became the first martyr of the war at the Boston Massacre. James Armistead's courageous espionage contributed to the fall of Cornwallis. George Washington's aide and companion throughout the war was William Lee. The bravery of black regiments, such as the Bucks of America, is noted. Some of the black men who fought were granted freedom and pensions. Many died in poverty without honor, however.

Fireworks, Picnics, and Flags:
The Story of the Fourth of July Symbols

Written by James Cross Giblin
Illustrated by Ursula Arndt
Clarion Books, 1983
90 pages, index

A summary of Revolutionary War history and the signing of the Declaration of Independence is followed by explanations of symbols associated with patriotism. These include brief histories of the flag, fireworks, Uncle Sam, the eagle, and the Liberty Bell. Special Fourth of July celebrations, the Centennial Exhibition of 1876, and the Bicentennial of 1976 are included. A list of important events that have taken place on July 4 over the years provides little-known facts of interest.

Give Us Liberty! The Story of the Declaration of Independence
Written by Helen Stone Peterson
Illustrated with black-and-white photographs
Garrard Publishing Company, 1973
96 pages, index

This clearly focused account of the history of the Declaration of Independence includes descriptions of the writing and editing by Thomas Jefferson and the committee, the debate and changes by the delegates to the Second Continental Congress, the voting for ratification, and the care and display of the document.

Privateers of Seventy-Six
Written by Fred J. Cook
Illustrated by William L. Verrill, Jr.
Bobbs-Merrill Company, Inc., 1976
174 pages

Lacking a well-equipped Continental navy, General Washington commissioned private ships, giving them authority to raid British ships. Individual colonies also granted commissions, and Benjamin Franklin engaged French privateers to support the cause. The efforts of these sea captains and crews contributed significantly to the outcome of the war. They captured large stores of weapons and ammunition for use by the Continental army, put many British ships out of service, and gained valuable goods for themselves and their fledgling country.

The Revolutionary War:
A Sourcebook on Colonial America
(American Albums from the Collections of the Library of Congress Series)
Edited by Carter Smith
Illustrated with black-and-white photographs and prints
The Millbrook Press, Inc., 1991
96 pages, index

Written in clear, understandable language and profusely illustrated, this book provides a good summary of major events of the war. The first part focuses on battles through 1776. This is followed by an explanation of the Declaration of Independence and events occurring through 1778. The conclusion of the war is covered in the third section. Each of the three parts has a detailed timeline of major events for the period covered.

The Story of the Boston Tea Party
Written by Mary Kay Phelan
Illustrated by Frank Aloise
Thomas Y. Crowell, 1973
113 pages, bibliography, index

This book is well focused on the events leading up to the Boston Tea Party and the major people involved in them. It describes the numerous efforts of the Patriots to convince the royal governor and tea agents to send ships back to England with tea still in their holds. Details about the actual opening of the chests and the dumping of tea into the harbor bring the event to life. Parliament's reaction and the consequences are briefly mentioned.

The War for Independence:
The Story of the American Revolution
Written by Albert Marrin
Illustrated with black-and-white photographs of famous paintings and prints
Atheneum, 1988
276 pages, maps, bibliography, index

A well-written, cogent account of the major events of the war, beginning with causes rooted in the French and Indian War and concluding with Washington's emotional farewell dinner with his officers. Important people and battles are described in context, presenting a balanced view of the motivations and beliefs of people with differing opinions. Propaganda perpetuated throughout the war is cited and placed in historical perspective. The war is examined from a variety of viewpoints, including battles at sea, conflicts on the frontier, and the contributions of spies on both sides.

The War We Could Have Lost: The American Revolution
Written by Clifford Lindsey Alderman
Illustrated with black-and-white photographs
Four Winds Press, 1974
224 pages, bibliography, index

All of the advantages were with the British as the war began. They had well-trained, experienced troops led by professional officers, plentiful supplies and ammunition, and valuable money backed by gold and silver. The blame for losing the war is laid on the generals (Gage, Howe, Burgoyne, Cornwallis, and Clinton) and

British government officials, including King George and incompetent cabinet members. Containing a plethora of specific details about major battles, this book cites numerous instances of missed opportunities, poor decisions, and outright blunders that aided the Americans and contributed to the British defeat.

Biographies

And Then What Happened, Paul Revere?
Written by Jean Fritz
Illustrated by Margot Tomes
Coward-McCann, Inc., 1973
48 pages

This brief account of Revere's life highlights his major accomplishments and provides a sense of his enthusiastic personality. Interesting details about his famous ride present anecdotal information in a humorous way. Author's notes at the end of the book provide additional factual information about major incidents mentioned in the story.

Benjamin Franklin: The New American
Written by Milton Meltzer
Illustrated with black-and-white photographs and prints
Franklin Watts, 1988
288 pages, bibliography, index

This scholarly work begins with Franklin's early life and his success as a printer. His retirement at age 42 enabled him to devote himself to scientific experiments and inventions and, later, to statesmanship. His role as a diplomat, first in England and later in France, contributed significantly to the emerging status of the United States. He played a major role in negotiating the peace at Versailles in 1783 and used his skills of compromise at the Constitutional Convention. This frank account gives full recognition to Franklin's many accomplishments, while including some of the controversial aspects of his life not generally found in books for young readers.

Can't You Make Them Behave, King George?
Written by Jean Fritz
Illustrated by Tomie de Paola
Coward, McCann & Geoghegan, Inc., 1977
48 pages

King George III is presented as a conscientious person who had learned the rules about being king well and wanted to perform his duties appropriately. Unfortunately, the colonialists in America were acting like obstinate children and were not recognizing his authority, especially regarding taxation to pay for losses in the French and Indian War and to maintain a British army in the colonies for their defense. He reluctantly signed the proclamation granting independence and regretted the loss of the American colonies for the rest of his life.

Deborah Sampson: Soldier of the Revolution
Written by Harold W. Felton
Illustrated by John Martinez
Dodd, Mead & Company, 1976
112 pages, index

Dressed as a man and enlisting under the name of Robert Shirtliff, Deborah Sampson is the only woman known to have served as a soldier in the Revolutionary War. She was recognized for her bravery and leadership qualities. She removed a bullet from her own leg and protected her identity by volunteering for outpost duty to avoid being in confined quarters. Her true identity was revealed when she became ill near the end of the war, and she was granted a military pension.

George Washington and the Birth of Our Nation
Written by Milton Meltzer
Illustrated with black-and-white photographs
Franklin Watts, 1986
188 pages, index

Penetrating behind myths and legends, Meltzer presents George Washington, the ordinary man, who was born into the middle class and married into aristocracy. Washington humbly accepted his thrust to greatness as commander in chief of the Continental army, fearing that his abilities and military experience might not be equal to the task. He reluctantly agreed to serve his new country as president, but was happiest when he could be at home on his beloved Mount Vernon.

Heroines of '76
Written by Elizabeth Anticaglia
Walker and Company, 1975
112 pages, glossary, bibliography

This volume honors 14 women who contributed to the American Revolution, either through actual fighting or by providing inspiration and support to the cause. Each chapter begins with a brief biographical sketch that is followed by a fictionalized version of an important event or events in the person's life.

The Many Lives of Benjamin Franklin
Written by Mary Pope Osborne
Illustrated with black-and-white photographs and prints
Dial Books for Young Readers, 1990
127 pages, bibliography, index

An interesting, readable account of Franklin's life, including his major accomplishments in printing, science, inventing, and statesmanship. A six-page list of one-sentence summaries of his major accomplishments closes with the fact that he was the only one of the Founding Fathers to sign all five of the great state papers that achieved our independence: the Declaration of Independence, the Treaty of Amity and Commerce with France, the Treaty of Alliance with France, the Treaty of Peace with England, and the Constitution of the United States. A timeline of important dates in Franklin's life is also included.

Patrick Henry
Written by Diana Reische
Illustrated with black-and-white photographs
Franklin Watts, 1987
92 pages, bibliography, index

Henry is presented as a logical, rational leader and a master orator. His famous cases and quotations are cited in historical context, including his victory in the Parson's Cause, his Stamp Act speech, and his famous Give me liberty or give me death! statement. He passionately promoted being an American as being more important than being from a specific colony. He was elected to the

First and Second Continental Congresses and to the governorship of Virginia.

Patriots in Petticoats
Written by Patricia Edwards Clyne
Illustrated by Richard Lebenson
Dodd, Mead & Company, 1976
144 pages, index

Contains 15 short biographies of women known for their bravery during the Revolutionary War. Historic mention of other women is also noted. The stories begin with the White Squaw of Kanawha, Anne Bailey, who recruited men for the army along the frontier. Lydia Darragh, Nancy Hart, Molly Pitcher, and Deborah Sampson are among the other women whose stories are recorded. Notes at the end of each chapter provide information about sites of historical markers dedicated to these brave women.

Phoebe and the General
Written by Judith Berry Griffin
Illustrated by Margot Tomes
Coward, McCann & Geoghegan, Inc., 1977
48 pages

The Queen's Head Tavern in New York City was a favorite meeting place for Patriots. Samuel Fraunces, the owner, was a free black man who supported General Washington. When he heard rumors of a plot to assassinate the General, he sent his 13-year-old daughter to act as a housekeeper and spy in Washington's New York residence. Phoebe's constant vigilance paid off. She discovered an attempt to poison Washington and identified the traitor, who was subsequently hanged.

Radical of the Revolution: Samuel Adams
Written by Margaret Green
Julian Messner, 1971
192 pages, bibliography, index

Sometimes called the single most powerful enemy of the British Empire, Samuel Adams devoted more than 30 years to his crusade for better representation of the common man in the affairs of government. When logic failed to sway the masses in Boston, he resorted to propaganda based on emotional appeal. He used every incident between the British and the colonies to his advantage, including the so-called Boston Massacre and the Boston Tea Party. He served as a delegate to the Continental Congress and as a member of the House of Representatives of Massachusetts, but his opposition to the Federalist party, which gained control of the new national government, deprived him of recognition in later years.

They Made a Revolution: 1776
Written by Jules Archer
St. Martin's Press, 1973
175 pages

A tribute to the theory that people rise to the challenge of the times, these biographies describe ten of the principal leaders of the American Revolution as human beings possessing the same strengths and weaknesses as all people. Reflecting on the war as the consequence of the revolution that occurred in the hearts and minds of the people between 1760 and 1775, the biographies focus on these people's lives before 7 June 1776, when Richard Henry Lee proposed to the delegates of the Second Continental Congress that they should declare themselves to be free and independent states. The book contains a list of the 56 signers of the Declaration of Independence by colony represented, including their ages, occupations, and some notes about how signing the document affected their lives.

Thomas Jefferson
(First Book Biography Series)
Written by Charles Patterson
Illustrated with black-and-white photographs
Franklin Watts, 1987
95 pages, bibliography, index

Jefferson's life from childhood to death is covered in an objective, forthright manner. His intellectual curiosity and his education in law provided a firm foundation for his many contributions to the birth and nurturing of the United States. In addition to writing the Declaration of Independence, he served as governor of Virginia, ambassador to France, secretary of state for George Washington, vice president with John Adams, and president of the United States for two terms. He then fulfilled a lifetime goal by founding the University of Virginia in Charlottesville.

Thomas Paine
(World Leaders Past & Present Series)
Written by John Vail
Illustrated with black-and-white photographs and prints
Chelsea House Publishers, 1990
112 pages, chronology, bibliography, index

The power of the printed word was dramatically exhibited by the pamphlets written by Paine. Raised in a Quaker household in England, he came to America in 1774 at the age of 37. *Common Sense*, his brilliant argument for independence and a republican form of government, was published in 1776. This pamphlet and *The Crisis*, the series of pamphlets that followed, rendered the complex issues of the time understandable for ordinary citizens. Paine returned to Europe in 1787 and participated in the French Revolution, which resulted in his imprisonment. He barely escaped death, and his health was broken when James Madison, ambassador to France, intervened for his release. Paine returned to the United States and died in obscurity seven years later.

Three for Revolution
Written by Burke Davis
Illustrated with prints and portraits of the period
Harcourt Brace Jovanovich, 1975
160 pages, bibliography, index

Three Myth-Encrusted Heroes from Virginia are presented as living human beings responding to the challenges of their times. The background of the changing land is described in the first chapter. Patrick Henry is likened to a trumpet in praise of his eloquent oratory. Thomas Jefferson's symbol is the pen, in recognition of his contribution in writing the Declaration of Independence. George Washington is portrayed as the sword. The biographies concentrate on the men's lives up to the summer of 1776. The last chapter summarizes their later years.

Traitor: The Case of Benedict Arnold
Written by Jean Fritz
G. P. Putnam's Sons, 1981
192 pages, bibliography, index

Arnold is portrayed as a short, cocky man obsessed with a need for attention and an ostentatious life-style. He entered the war enthusiastically, was a hero in battle many times, and was known to be a favorite of General Washington. After suffering a crippling injury that left him with one leg shorter than the other, he married Tory sympathizer Peggy Shippon and decided he could help end the war more quickly if he aided the British by giving them control of West Point. His plan failed, but he was granted asylum by the British and, in fact, led some battles against the Patriots. He finished out his life in England, never understanding why he was so generally hated by both Tories and Patriots, or why his name had become synonymous with the word *traitor.*

What's the Big Idea, Ben Franklin?
Written by Jean Fritz
Illustrated by Margot Tomes
Coward-McCann, Inc., 1976
48 pages

Franklin is portrayed as energetic and inquisitive. He did not like the idea of apprenticeships, refusing his father's suggestions until he reluctantly agreed to serve as a printer's helper with his brother. Learning the business quickly, Franklin left Boston for Philadelphia before his apprenticeship was completed. The book includes Franklin's experiments with electricity and some of his inventions, as well as efforts to influence the English government during his 18 years in that country and his success in obtaining France's support in the war.

Where Was Patrick Henry on the 29th of May?
Written by Jean Fritz
Illustrated by Margot Tomes
Coward, McCann & Geoghegan, Inc., 1975
48 pages

Patrick Henry is portrayed as a carefree youth growing up in the backwoods of Virginia in the 1700s. His failures at farming and in business are mentioned, as are his two marriages and 15 children. He became a lawyer, and his great speaking ability was discovered when he pleaded a case to allow colonial governments to decide how much to pay parsons. His other significant speeches are also mentioned.

Why Don't You Get a Horse, Sam Adams?

Written by Jean Fritz
Illustrated by Trina Schart Hyman
Coward, McCann & Geoghegan, Inc., 1974
48 pages

Focusing on little-known facts about Adams, Fritz provides a humanistic and humorous perspective of one of the major forces behind the revolution. Adams is presented as a short, mild-mannered man who cared nothing about his appearance. He walked the streets of Boston daily, talking against the king and British rule. When his cousin John Adams finally convinced him to try riding a horse, he could only do so when he wore padded underpants to ease the bumpy ride.

Will You Sign Here, John Hancock?

Written by Jean Fritz
Illustrated by Trina Schart Hyman
Coward-McCann, Inc., 1976
48 pages

As the richest man in New England, John Hancock was accustomed to the best of everything. His fancy style of dress and his elaborate parties caused him to be noticed by everyone, including King George, who placed Hancock on his Dangerous Americans list with a price on his head. As president of the Second Continental Congress, Hancock was the first to sign the Declaration of Independence, which he did with a flourish befitting his style and vanity.

Yankee Doodle Boy: A Young Soldier's Adventures in the American Revolution Told by Himself

Written by Joseph Plumb Martin
Edited by George F. Scheer
Illustrated by Victor Mays
William R. Scott, Inc., 1964
191 pages, maps, index

Fifteen-year-old Joseph Martin joined the Continental army in 1776 for a six-month hitch and served for seven long years. He described his ordeal as a private in an underpaid and underprovisioned army many years later. His memoirs vividly portray the times that not only tried men's souls, but their bodies too. The soldiers constantly suffered from hunger and exposure to the elements. They ate horses, dogs, tree bark, and their own shoes. Most nights were spent attempting to sleep on the ground without blankets or protection from rain, frost, or other inclement weather. Martin's matter-of-fact presentation and his sense of humor reveal both the joys and tribulations of the common fighting man.

Fiction Books

Early Thunder
Written by Jean Fritz
Illustrated by Lynd Ward
Coward-McCann, Inc., 1967
255 pages

Fourteen-year-old Daniel West was a Tory opposed to the cruel and vicious actions of the Liberty Boys in Salem. His family was frequently the recipient of the gifts these people left on Tory doorsteps during the night, such as piles of garbage, rotten eggs, or manure. Eventually Daniel began to question his loyalty to the king and began to see some merit in the values expressed by the Patriots. When a showdown occurred between the British regulars and the Salem townspeople, he thwarted British attempts to take his boat and loudly proclaimed his allegiance to the Whigs. The story is based on an actual incident that took place in Salem in 1775 and includes references to historical people of the time.

The Fighting Ground
Written by Avi
J. B. Lippincott, 1984
157 pages

Thirteen-year-old Jonathan was angry with his father for not allowing him to join the army. When he is unexpectedly summoned, he discovers that the reality of war is much different from the glamour he imagined fighting for freedom would bring. Captured by Hessians, he finds out what war is really like as he struggles for his life. The minute-by-minute account of his 24 hours as a soldier presents a realistic sense of the experience of war.

The Griffin Legacy
Written by Jan O'Donnell Klaveness
Macmillan Publishing Company, 1983
184 pages

The long-term effects of Patriot hatred for Tories during the revolutionary period is exemplified in this story of a teenage girl who is called to solve a mystery over a century and a half old. Amy is pulled into the romance of an ancestor and her suitor, a church rector who remained loyal to England during the war. He was killed and buried in disgrace outside the churchyard. The spirits of her relative as a young girl and of the rector appear to Amy, imploring her to find the documents and artifacts that will correct historical errors.

Guns for General Washington:
A Story of the American Revolution
Written by Seymour Reit
Gulliver Books, Harcourt Brace Jovanovich, 1990
98 pages, bibliography

Based on an actual incident, the great cannon trek of 1775, this story chronicles the dangers of moving several tons of heavy artillery hundreds of miles from Fort Ticonderoga in New York to Boston. The valiant journey across lakes and rivers, over mountains, and through ice and snow successfully provided Washington's troops with the artillery needed to force the British to evacuate Boston.

Johnny Tremain
Written by Esther Forbes
Illustrated by Lynd Ward
Houghton Mifflin Company, 1943
256 pages

Johnny's goal of becoming a master silversmith appears to be shattered when he accidently injures his hand with molten silver. He wanders aimlessly around Boston until he meets Rab in a printer's shop and finds both a friend and a job. Rab is a Patriot and Johnny gradually becomes a part of the movement, interacting with such well-known people as John Hancock, Paul Revere, and Sam Adams. He participates in the Boston Tea Party, carries messages, and observes the repercussions of the first few days of fighting.

Jump Ship to Freedom
Written by James Lincoln Collier and Christopher Collier
Delacorte Press, 1981
198 pages

Daniel Arabus's father had earned his freedom from slavery by fighting in the war in place of his master. He had saved his pay of $600 in Continental notes to buy the freedom of his son and wife, but the notes were worthless unless the Constitutional Convention could work out their differences and form a national government. Then Daniel's father dies in a shipwreck, and it is up to Daniel to rescue the notes from his unscrupulous master and escape from his tyranny if there is to be any chance of buying his own and his mother's freedom. His perilous journey takes him from Connecticut to New York and then to Philadelphia, where he delivers an important message to William Samuel Johnson.

My Brother Sam Is Dead
Written by James Lincoln Collier and Christopher Collier
Four Winds Press, 1974
216 pages

Tim does not know whether to side with the Patriots or the Tories. His older brother Sam has left Yale to join the Continental army, but his father is totally opposed to war and is accused of being a Tory. Tim wishes this was a normal argument with two sides instead of a complex problem with about six sides. His father is captured and later dies on a prison ship. When Sam's regiment is quartered just outside of town, Tim and his mother enjoy seeing him occasionally. During one of his visits a cow is stolen from their barn, and when Sam rushes out to stop them, the robbers accuse him of the crime. Anxious to make an example of soldiers who steal from townspeople, General Putnam sentences Sam to execution. Although the main characters are fictitious, the location in Connecticut was an actual Tory township, and several of the secondary characters are based on real people.

Sarah Bishop
Written by Scott O'Dell
Houghton Mifflin Company, 1980
184 pages

Sarah, a teenage girl, is left to fend for herself when her family's small farm is burned and her Tory father dies as a result of being tarred and feathered. Sarah attempts to find her brother, who has joined the Continental army, but discovers he has died aboard a prisoner of war ship. This story vividly portrays both the dangers and the joys of surviving in the wilderness of Long Island.

The Secret of Van Rink's Cellar
Written by Beverly Haskell Lee
Lerner Publications Company, 1979
174 pages

Sara and her brother are not prepared for the startling discovery that their quiet mother is a spy for the Patriots. When their mother becomes sick, they attempt to continue conveying her messages, but they do not realize the danger of such a mission. A map of the New York region at the time of the American Revolution aids in following the action of the story.

War Comes to Willy Freeman
Written by James Lincoln Collier and Christopher Collier
Delacorte Press, 1983
178 pages

When 13-year-old Willy's father is killed in an attack on Fort Griswold and her mother is taken prisoner by the British, she is suddenly left on her own. As a free young black girl, she knows she is in jeopardy. Disguised as a boy, she sets off for New York to look for her mother. She works in the Fraunces Tavern to support herself during her search, which ends when Willy finds her mother on her deathbed. Woven into the narrative are facts about Jack Arabus, a freed slave who fought in the Revolutionary War and won his case in a Connecticut court to avoid being taken back into slavery.

Sample Lesson Plan

Introduction

Read the poem "Paul Revere's Ride" by Henry Wadsworth Longfellow aloud to the class. Discuss why Longfellow wrote the poem. Then make a list of "facts" the students know about the Revolutionary War and another list of questions they would like to answer on chart paper or transparencies.

Building Background

Meet in the library media center. Ask each student to work with a partner to find as many causes for the American Revolution as possible. They may use library books, computer programs, encyclopedias, and other reference materials to locate information. The school librarian may provide the students instruction or review in using these sources before they begin. Students may also need instruction in ways to record information. The webbing technique or another note-taking process may be taught in either the classroom or in the library.

Have each pair of students meet with another pair and combine their lists of causes. Then meet as a total class and make a composite list of causes on chart paper or transparencies.

Issues

Seeds of the Revolution in Boston

Discuss the situation in Boston from the conclusion of the French and Indian War until the beginning of the Revolutionary War. Meet in the library media center to find answers to the following questions: In what ways did the seeds of the revolution thrive in Boston? Who were the instigators and leaders? Why were the Stamp Act Congress and the First and Second Continental Congresses held? Who were the participants?

Meet as a class to share information found; record pertinent facts on chart paper or transparencies.

Declaration of Independence

Read aloud the preamble and the statement of rights from the Declaration of Independence. Talk about their meaning and why they were written. Could war have been avoided before this point? Was it inevitable after this point? Did all of the colonists agree with the Declaration? What happened to people who chose to remain loyal to Great Britain?

Distribute copies of the Declaration of Independence so students may read the list of charges against King George III as they participate in the discussion.

Major Battles and Turning Points

Discuss the fighting at Lexington and Concord and the beginning of the war. Divide the class into three groups. One group will research battles and activities in the North, another in the South, and the third along the western frontier.

Discuss the war battles and activities. Bring out the list of "facts" and questions generated in the introduction. Which statements have been found to be true? Which have been found to be false? Which questions still need answers?

Projects

Distribute a list of possible projects. (See suggested activities with this unit and general activities in the Introduction for ideas.) Ask students to choose one. More than one could be completed for extra credit. Students may work on chosen projects in the classroom and school library as appropriate. Projects may be shared during a class session or placed on display during the Return to the Revolutionary Era Event, which is described below.

Fiction Books

Distribute a list of available fiction books. Ask each student to choose one to read and critically analyze in a written paper. This paper should include an evaluation of literary qualities (see Appendix B for suggested guidelines) and a summary of the insights about the war gained through reading the book.

Divide students into groups of four or five; each student in each group should have read a different fiction book. Have small group discussions based on the variety of perspectives presented in the books and analyses of literary qualities. Pull the class together near the end of the session to share insights as a large group.

Effects of the War

Discuss the short-term and long-term results of the war. Where were the peace talks held? Who attended? What were the terms of the agreement? In what ways were the former colonies prepared to be independent? What were some of their problems in dealing with independence?

Return to the Revolutionary Era Event

Read some of the selections from Leonard Everett Fisher's *Picture Book of Revolutionary War Heroes* aloud. Ask students to begin thinking about which person they would like to study and impersonate for the Return to the Revolutionary Era Event at the conclusion of the unit.

Guidelines for the Event

- Each student will select one person to research and impersonate.
- Information may be found in classroom resources, the school library, and public libraries.
- Students are encouraged to seek information from current sources, such as professors of American history at nearby colleges and universities or from libraries that have special collections of the person's papers or works. They may access this information through letters and telephone calls. (Students may need instruction in writing business letters and conducting interviews.)
- Each student will make a chart about the revolutionary era person. This chart will include important dates and events in the person's life. It may be illustrated with drawings or copies of appropriate pictures. (Students may need some instruction in layout and lettering. Art teachers may be willing to help.)
- Each student will prepare or acquire a costume approximating the person's style of dress as closely as possible. Hairstyles or wigs can contribute to the characterization.
- Each student will prepare a list of ten appropriate questions for an interviewer to ask of the Revolutionary era person.

Meet in the school library. Ask students to look for further information about people they would like to study. A list of possibilities may be distributed. Have each student turn in a list of three choices at the end of the class period; this will enable the teacher and librarian to make assignments that will allow each student to study a different person.

Note: Because of the social circumstances of the time, women's roles were generally more limited and less influential than men's, so some girls may choose to study and impersonate men. Also, keep in mind that the event will be more interesting if infamous and little-known people are included as well as patriots and heroes. Consider including Benedict Arnold, King George III, and Martha Washington, for instance.

Announce assignments for the Return to the Revolutionary Era Event. This will be an ongoing project and the culminating activity for the unit.

Culminating Activity

The Return to the Revolutionary Era Event may be an in-class activity or an evening activity for parents and the public. Students come dressed as the Revolutionary era person they have studied. They impersonate these people throughout the event answering questions as these people would have answered them.

Formal Program

Characters approach a microphone one at a time and an interviewer, such as a school principal, school board member, or other dignitary, asks questions based on those the students have prepared as part of the assignment.

Another possibility is to have groups of about four characters serve as panels of experts on the war. The moderator asks questions or suggests topics for discussion.

A display of students' charts and memorabilia about the characters may be set up in a nearby open area or in classrooms.

Informal Program

The characters are arranged around the perimeter of a large room, such as a gymnasium, with their charts and memorabilia close by. Guests visit each of them to ask questions. Questions may be posted beside the characters or distributed as a handout.

Combination of Formal and Informal Program

A formal program of short interviews of two or three questions for each character may be followed by informal viewing and visiting.

Suggested Questions

Why do some authors and scholars refer to the Revolutionary War as our First Civil War?

How had space and time set the colonies apart from England?

How did the social structure and cultural values of the colonists and the British differ?

At what points during the ongoing disagreements could either the colonists or the British have made different decisions that could have avoided war?

What are some of the crimes George Washington would have been charged with if the colonies had lost the war and he had been tried for treason?

Was the Boston Massacre really a massacre? Why was it referred to in this language in the writings of the time?

What propaganda techniques did Samuel Adams use to increase public support for the need for independence from England?

Why did Bostonians refuse to buy tea from the British East India Company when it was less expensive than the tea they were purchasing from Holland?

How did Thomas Paine's *Common Sense* contribute to the war effort?

Why did the Tories remain loyal to Great Britain? What percentage of the colonists were estimated to be Tories?

Why were privateers commissioned to attack British ships at sea?

Why did German soldiers fight for the British?

Which foreign countries helped the colonies during the war? What were their motives?

How did the status of the American Indians change as a result of the war?

In what ways was the Revolutionary War more than a conflict between Great Britain and her colonies?

Suggested Activities

Make a list of the proclamations and acts passed by Parliament between 1763 and 1776 that levied taxes on the colonists and restricted their rights.

Write a justification for British taxation of the colonies from King George's point of view.

Dramatize Charles Townshend's presentation of his proposals to Parliament for taxation of the colonies.

Brainstorm solutions other than war to the problems between England and the colonies. Construct a chart of solutions that would not have involved war, listing for each one the advantages and disadvantages from each side's point of view.

Make a list of famous quotations from the Revolutionary War era. Include the names of people credited with the quotations and the dates.

Reenact the Boston Tea Party, including the meetings prior to the dumping of tea in the harbor.

Reenact the editing and revising of the Declaration of Independence when the writing committee met with Thomas Jefferson before the document was presented to the Second Continental Congress.

Dramatize the debate that could have taken place in one of the colonial legislatures in deciding whether or not to ratify the Declaration of Independence.

Write a diary that George Washington or one of the other military leaders could have kept during the war.

Dramatize Deborah Sampson's enlistment in the Continental army.

Write an obituary (not to exceed 150 words) for one or more of the notable people of the Revolutionary War period.

Create a picture book of patriotic symbols, such as the flag, the eagle, and the Liberty Bell.

Make a list of ways the Fourth of July is celebrated across the country. Mention special celebrations for the centennial and bicentennial anniversaries.

Compose a song that could have been sung by Continental soldiers.

Create an almanac based on Franklin's *Poor Richard's Almanac.*

Glossary

Articles of Confederation—Regulations for ruling the colonies until the end of the war. Adopted by the Second Continental Congress on 15 November 1777, but did not go into effect until 1781 after being ratified by all of the colonies.

Boston Massacre—The killing of five colonists by British soldiers during a mob fight. During the ensuing trial, the soldiers were found to have been acting in self-defense.

Boston Tea Party—Liberty Boys dressed as Indians boarded three English ships and threw the cargoes of tea into the harbor to protest the tax on tea.

Caucus Club—An organization in Boston in the 1730s that met to discuss ways for better government representation of the working man. Samuel Adams' father was one of the founders.

committees of correspondence—Organized by Boston Patriots to inform other colonies and countries about British abuses of American rights and liberties, thus keeping the spirit of rebellion alive.

Common Sense—A 42-page pamphlet written by Thomas Paine that advocated a call for declaring independence from Great Britain.

Daughters of Liberty—Women who supported the resistance of Britain's taxation by boycotting British goods such as tea and cloth.

Declaration of Independence—A document adopted by the Second Continental Congress listing grievances against King George III and claiming the right of the colonies to be free and independent.

Declaratory Act—Passed in 1766 when the Stamp Act was repealed, proclaiming full British authority over the American colonies.

effigy—An image or a representation of a person. Some well-known Tories were burned in effigy.

First Continental Congress—Delegates from every colony except Georgia gathered in Philadelphia in September 1774 to denounce the Intolerable Acts and establish procedures for enforcing the boycott against British goods.

Hessians—German soldiers hired by the British.

Intolerable Acts—The British ended self-government in Massachusetts and closed Boston Harbor in retaliation for the Boston Tea Party.

Liberty Boys—Men who met, sometimes secretly, to formulate plans for achieving independent rule in the colonies.

Liberty Tree—A tree in a large open common in Boston. The common was often used as a meeting place for Whig gatherings.

Loyalists—Colonists who remained loyal to King George III. Some joined forces with the redcoats and fought against the Patriots.

mercenaries—Soldiers paid to fight battles for another country, such as the Hessians who fought for Great Britain.

militiamen—Colonial citizen-soldiers who owned their own muskets and drilled on village greens to practice their military skills.

minutemen—Colonial volunteers who promised to be ready for military duty at a minute's notice.

musket—A heavy, large-caliber, shoulder firearm.

Navigation Acts—Forbade the colonies to trade with countries other than England.

Parliament—England's legislative body.

Patriots—People who believed that the colonies had a right to declare their independence from Great Britain.

Proclamation of 1763—Recognized Indians as owners of lands they occupied. Closed lands west of the Allegheny Mountains to further settlement or colonization.

Quartering Act—Required colonial authorities to provide quarters, fuel, candles, cider or beer, and transportation for British troops stationed in the colonies.

redcoat—Name for a British soldier taken from the red uniform he wore.

Restraining Act—Forbade the colonies to trade with any country other than Great Britain and the islands of the British West Indies.

Second Continental Congress—A meeting of representatives from the 13 colonies held in Philadelphia beginning in June 1775 to create an American army and debate independence. George Washington was elected commander in chief.

sedition—Incitement of resistance against lawful authority.

Sons of Liberty—Began as groups of men who resisted the Stamp Act and became the term used for Patriots opposed to British rule.

Stamp Act—An act passed by Parliament in 1765 and repealed in 1766 requiring colonists to purchase stamps for all legal documents and newspapers.

Stamp Act Congress—Delegates from nine colonies met in New York, demonstrating the first suggestion of colonial unity.

Sugar Act—Increased the tax on molasses from the French and British West Indies.

tar and feather—Tar was poured over a person's body followed by the contents of a feather pillow. Victims often suffered permanent disabilities, insanity, or death as a result.

Tea Act—Reduced the price of tea from the British East India Company, but retained the tax.

Tories—Colonists who remained loyal to King George III. Some joined forces with the redcoats and fought against the Patriots.

Townshend Acts—An act passed by Parliament in 1767 that placed heavy duties on many British goods coming into American ports.

Treaty of Paris—Document signed in 1783 declaring the United States to be a free and independent country. It also granted the new country land west to the Mississippi and protected its shipping and fishing rights.

Whigs—Name given to those Americans who resisted the British and came to support independence.

Civil War Literature Unit

Selected Chronology

1619	Twenty black Africans were brought to the colonies by a Dutch merchant ship and sold in Jamestown, Virginia.
1801	A law was passed by Congress preventing ship captains from bringing cargoes of black Africans to United States ports for sale as slaves.
1820	Missouri Compromise was passed—Missouri entered the Union as a slave state and Maine entered as a free state.
1845	Texas admitted to the Union as a slave state.
1848	Treaty ending War with Mexico brought many new territories in the Southwest under U.S. control.
1850	Compromise of 1850 passed by Congress, temporarily settling the debate over whether the new territories taken from Mexico should be slave or free.
1852	Publication of Uncle Tom's Cabin by Harriet Beecher Stowe.
1854	Fugitive slave Anthony Burns arrested in Boston under the Fugitive Slave Act passed as part of the Compromise of 1850. Kansas-Nebraska Act passed by Congress. The Republican party was founded.
1856	Armed conflict erupted between proslave and antislave forces in the Kansas Territory—known as "Bleeding Kansas."
1857	Dred Scott Decision in the Supreme Court.
1858	The Lincoln-Douglas debates held in Illinois.
1859	John Brown's raid at Harper's Ferry.

1860		Democratic party split into Northern and Southern branches.
	November	Abraham Lincoln elected president of the United States.
	December	South Carolina seceded from the United States.
1861	February	Conference of the Confederate States of America met in Montgomery, Alabama, to adopt a constitution and select Jefferson Davis as president.
	March 4	Abraham Lincoln inaugurated as president of the United States.
	April 12	Confederate troops attacked Fort Sumter.
	April 15	President Lincoln issued a call for troops.
	April 19	Lincoln proclaimed a blockade of the South.
	May	The Confederate capital was moved to Richmond, Virginia.
	July	First major battle of the War fought at Bull Run.
1862	March	First battle of ironclad ships: the Virginia (also known as the Merrimack) and the Monitor.
1863	January 1	The Emancipation Proclamation of President Lincoln freed all slaves in Confederate-held territory.
	May–July	Seige at Vicksburg.
	July	Battle of Gettysburg.
	July 4	Vicksburg surrendered to General Grant.
	July	Draft riots in New York.
	November	Lincoln delivered the Gettysburg Address at the dedication of a soldiers' cemetery in Gettysburg.
1864	March	General Grant named commander-in-chief of U.S. forces.
	November 8	Abraham Lincoln reelected president of the United States.
1865	April 9	General Lee surrendered to General Grant at Appomattox Courthouse in Virginia.
	April 14	Abraham Lincoln was assassinated.

Recommended Books

Picture Books

Cecil's Story
Written by George Ella Lyon
Illustrated with paintings by Peter Catalanotto
Orchard Books, 1991
32 pages

A what if story presents a young boy thinking about what it would be like to have his father go to war and his mother leave to bring the injured father back. The boy stays with neighbors and worries until his parents return. Although his father has lost an arm, he is still his dad and he's glad he's back.

Nettie's Trip South
Written by Ann Turner
Illustrated by Ronald Himler
Macmillan Publishing Company, 1987
30 pages

Inspired by a diary kept by her great-grandmother in 1859, Turner has presented some of the memorable images of the slave trade as witnessed by a ten-year-old child. Attending a Negro auction nauseated her at the time and caused her to become an avowed abolitionist for the rest of her life.

Thunder at Gettysburg
Written by Patricia Lee Gauch
Illustrated by Stephen Gammell
G. P. Putnam's Sons, [1975] 1990
48 pages

Tillie Pierce Alleman was excited about the battle that seemed to be getting started within easy viewing distance, but she discovered the terror of war as the fighting surrounded the farmhouse she was visiting. Written in terse, condensed prose, the narrative provides a firsthand experience of being caught in the war. Based on a true incident.

The Vicksburg Veteran
Written by F. N. Monjo
Illustrated by Douglas Gorsline
Simon & Schuster, Inc., 1971
62 pages

General Grant's 12-year-old son accompanied him to the Battle of Vicksburg. The book is written in diary form as Fred might have kept track of his adventures. Although the diary is fictionalized, the events from 16 April to 4 July 1863, are based on actual facts.

Who Owns the Sun
Written and illustrated by Stacy Chbosky
Landmark Editions, Inc., 1988
29 pages

In this beautifully illustrated book, a young boy asks his father many questions about the earth and the sky and who owns them. His father always answers that the beautiful things of the world were placed here to be loved and appreciated by all. One day the boy overhears a conversation in which he learns that his father is owned by a man. In response to the boy's anguished questioning, the father replies that the man owns his body, but he cannot own his heart and mind. It is only at this point that the reader realizes the father and son are slaves.

Factual Books

The Battle of Gettysburg
Written by Neil Johnson
Illustrated with photographs from the 125th anniversary reenactment of the battle
Four Winds Press, 1989
56 pages, bibliography

The author participated in the reenactment of the Battle of Gettysburg as an official photographer, taking pictures that captured the sense of living history. Thousands of serious Civil War students reenacted three of the major battles, one for each day. A balanced presentation in the text summarizes the background of the battle and the actual fighting, reflecting respect for the leaders and soldiers on both sides.

The Battle of Gettysburg: 1–3 July 1863
Written and illustrated by Ian Ribbons
Oxford University Press, 1974
80 pages, maps

A brief background of the war's beginning is given on the first few pages. The majority of the book is devoted to an hour-by-hour description of the three-day battle. Detailed illustrations and maps show the weapons used, the soldiers' uniforms, the types of dwellings inhabited, and the movements of troops. Inserts of newspaper articles and eyewitness reports add immediacy to the text.

Behind the Blue and Gray: Soldier's Life in the Civil War
(Young Readers' History of the Civil War Series)
Written by Delia Ray
Illustrated with black-and-white photographs
Lodestar Books, 1991
102 pages, glossary, bibliography, index

The perspective of common soldiers from both sides is presented. These young men generally had little experience of the world beyond their homes when they marched into battle. In mismatched uniforms and led by unseasoned officers, they were unprepared for the shock of death and horrible injury. Amputations were common and diseases claimed as many lives as battle. Deplorable prison conditions are vividly described. Problems with recruiting as the war dragged on, the need for draft laws, and the unethical behavior of potential recruits are also discussed. The contributions of blacks, both as soldiers and servants, are noted. The book closes with some of the devastating aftermath the war left for many survivors.

The Boys' War: Confederate and Union Soldiers Talk about the Civil War
Written by Jim Murphy
Illustrated with black-and-white photographs
Clarion Books, 1990
110 pages, bibliography, index

Many Civil War soldiers from both sides were between the ages of 12 and 19. Their role in the war is discussed, emphasizing their significant contributions. Most entered as innocent young men looking for glamour and adventure. The battles and hardships quickly caused them to become seasoned soldiers. Special recognition is given to drummer boys who were vital to the communication systems. The dismal conditions of prisons and hospitals are described. Frequent quotations from young men's letters and diaries make the war seem very personal.

The Civil War
(America at War Series)
Written by Michael Golay
Illustrated with black-and-white photographs
Facts on File, 1992
180 pages, bibliography, index

This comprehensive account begins with a summary of events leading up to the war. A detailed history of the conflict over slavery, including the work of such abolitionists as John Brown and Frederick Douglass, provides insights into the problems. Explanations of the selection and leadership qualities of the generals for both sides contribute to the detailed descriptions of the battles and use of sea power. Hardships endured by the citizens at home and the confusion resulting from the Emancipation Proclamation reveal the widespread impact of the war. The lack of medical knowledge about diseases and injuries caused more deaths than the fighting. The Battle of Gettysburg, the Siege of Vicksburg, the Battle of Chattanooga, and Sherman's march through Georgia are among the major events covered in some detail. The meeting of Generals Grant and Lee at Appomattox is followed by an epilogue describing the devastating aftermath of the war.

The Civil War and Reconstruction: An Eyewitness History
Written by Joe H. Kirchberger
Illustrated with black-and-white photographs and prints
Facts on File, 1991
389 pages, maps, bibliography, index

This oversize book contains ten chapters, beginning with the Missouri Compromise and concluding with the Reconstruction. Each chapter includes a brief summary of historical context, a detailed chronicle of events, and a selection of quotations from eyewitness accounts. A wide range of viewpoints is presented.

Four appendixes contain documents, a list of major battles, biographies of major personalities, and maps.

The Illustrated Confederate Reader
Written by Rod Gragg
Illustrated with black-and-white photographs
Harper & Row Publishers, 1989
291 pages, bibliography, index

Firsthand experiences of Southern soldiers and civilians are captured in their personal accounts of the war as found in diaries, letters, and other written accounts from the time. Gragg has connected these writings with brief narratives that depict the historical setting. In most cases, he mentions whether or not the writer or speaker survived the ordeal described. Various aspects of the war are included, such as everyday military life, prison camps, and Sherman's march of destruction.

John Brown and the Fight against Slavery
(Gateway Civil Rights Series)
Written by James L. Collins
Illustrated with black-and-white and color photographs and prints
Millbrook Press, 1991
32 pages, chronology, bibliography, index

The major events in Brown's life are described: his childhood with parents who hated slavery, his two marriages and 20 children, his obsession with abolishing slavery, his attack on Harper's Ferry, and his death by execution. Other abolitionists, such as Harriet Tubman, Harriet Beecher Stowe, and Henry Ward Beecher, and some history of the movement, including some of the major compromises and the Dred Scott case, are included.

The Long Road to Gettysburg
Written by Jim Murphy
Illustrated with black-and-white photographs
Clarion Books, 1992
116 pages, maps, bibliography, index

Based heavily on the war journals of Confederate Lieutenant John Dooley and Union Corporal Thomas Galway, this account presents a balanced view of the conflict from both sides and lends a personal sense to the long, exhausting marches; terrible, thunderous battles; and the shocking aftermath of mass death. The battles are described from a broader viewpoint as well. The contemporary lack of enthusiasm for Lincoln's brief Gettysburg address is also noted.

A Nation Torn: The Story of How the Civil War Began
Written by Delia Ray
Illustrated with black-and-white photographs
Lodestar Books, Dutton, 1990
102 pages, glossary, bibliography, index

Focusing on the background and causes of the war, this account begins and ends with the attack on Fort Sumter. Contrasting the life-styles and economies of the North and South shows the depth of their differences. Slavery, the most emotional issue, is dealt with in a balanced way, presenting both sides. Attempts at peaceful solutions, such as the Missouri Compromise and the Kansas-Nebraska Act, are discussed. Lincoln's involvement in seeking political offices and his election as president are a prelude to the secession of the Southern states and the beginning of the war.

A Separate Battle: Women and the Civil War
Written by Ina Chang
Illustrated with black-and-white photographs
Lodestar Books, 1991
103 pages, bibliography, index

Presenting the woman's point of view of the war, this book begins and ends with Angelina Grimke, a wealthy daughter of the South, who expressed disgust with slavery and moved to the North before the war. Women's roles in providing supplies and nursing care for soldiers, fighting disguised as men, and supporting the war effort in other ways are included. Contributions of both Northern and Southern women are presented.

This Hallowed Ground:
The Story of the Union Side of the Civil War
Written by Bruce Catton
Illustrated with black-and-white and color photographs and prints
Doubleday & Company, Inc., 1962
189 pages, maps, index
This book presents a comprehensive study of the war from the Union viewpoint, discussing major battles and the generals who led them. Frustrations and hardships of the common soldiers are included. The confused state of the country at the time of Lincoln's death is described, but the book ends on a note of hope.

Voices from the Civil War:
A Documentary History of the Great American Conflict
Edited by Milton Meltzer
Illustrated with contemporary prints
Thomas Y. Crowell, 1989
203 pages, bibliography, index
A firsthand sense of the war is offered through a mosaic of writings selected from such sources as letters, diaries, speeches, interviews, memoirs, and newspaper articles. Meltzer's brief passages set the stage for each entry and provide a sense of continuity for the narrative, which begins at the close of the Mexican War (with the controversy about whether new states would be slave or nonslave) and continues through the beginning of Reconstruction in the South.

Biographies

Anthony Burns: The Defeat and Triumph of a Fugitive Slave
Written by Virginia Hamilton
Alfred A. Knopf, 1988
193 pages, bibliography, index
Hamilton's historical reconstruction of one man's struggle for liberty is based on Anthony Burns' 1854 trial in Boston. Arrested under the Fugitive Slave Act, Burns became the center of violent turmoil as abolitionists and slaveholders waged their bitter fight. Chapters based on the trial are interspersed with flashbacks into Burns' childhood and his plans for escape. The slave owner was granted his right of property in the trial. He immediately trans-

ported Burns back to the South and placed him in prison. The inhumane conditions of his confinement broke Burns' health. Even though he was later purchased by abolitionists and set free, he died at the age of 28.

Behind Rebel Lines:
The Incredible Story of Emma Edmonds, Civil War Spy
Written by Seymour Reit
Gulliver Books, Harcourt Brace Jovanovich, 1988
102 pages, bibliography

Canadian-born Edmonds joined the Union army as Pvt. Franklin Thompson and began her distinguished career working in a tent hospital. Although her major disguise was not discovered, her ability to impersonate others was. She became a valued spy, slipping behind Confederate lines as a slave, peddler, washerwoman, and fop. She secured vital information for the Union cause in each of these roles.

Clara Barton
(American Women of Achievement Series)
Written by Leni Hamilton
Illustrated with black-and-white photographs and prints
Chelsea House Publishers, 1988
112 pages, chronology, bibliography, index

Clara Barton began her career as a schoolteacher at the age of 17 and founded an extremely successful school for paupers in her home state of Massachusetts. She then became the first woman employee of the federal government, working for the Patent Office. She was in Washington, D.C., when the Civil War started and immediately set about to bring aid and comfort to the soldiers. (There were no nursing schools in the United States prior to the Civil War. All nurses were self-taught and served without pay.) Clara's first supplies were sent at her request from the state of Massachusetts, but eventually her work was recognized and she administered tons of supplies for the Union government. Barton traveled to the front lines throughout the war to relieve suffering and hunger. After the war she became the founder of the Red Cross in the United States and served as its president for 23 years. She instigated the expansion of the organization's purpose to aid victims of disaster as well as of war.

Escape from Slavery: Five Journeys to Freedom
Written by Doreen Rappaport
Illustrated by Charles Lilly
HarperCollins Publishers, 1991
117 pages, bibliography

Focusing on escapes that featured individual acts of courage by slaves determined to be free, this book contains realistic portrayals of five escapes based on historical records. Crossing a melting river of ice, being shipped out in a cramped box, and donning disguises to travel by train are some examples of ways black people managed to leave the South and find freedom in the North.

Go Free or Die: A Story about Harriet Tubman
Written by Jeri Ferris
Illustrated by Karen Ritz
Carolrhoda Books, Inc., 1988
64 pages

This story focuses on the hardships of Tubman's childhood and her lifelong ambition to be free. Her refusal to bow to her owner was generally ignored because she was such a hard worker. With the help of her father, she learned the necessary skills for survival in preparation for her run for freedom. She was almost 30 years old when the opportunity came. After escaping, she returned to the South 19 times and helped over 300 slaves to freedom.

The Iron Will of Jefferson Davis
Written by Cass Canfield
Illustrated with black-and-white photographs
Harcourt Brace Jovanovich, 1978
146 pages, maps, bibliography, index

This sympathetic portrayal of Davis presents him as a compassionate, self-controlled man who had learned to suppress his emotions and his temper at an early age. A graduate of West Point, he eventually entered politics and served as a U.S. Senator. When the Confederate government was organized, he neither sought nor wanted the presidency, but was chosen because his moderate views were acceptable to both the radical and pro-Union factions. He was actually not well qualified or well suited for the job. Much of the book is devoted to specific battles of the war with emphasis on problems caused by lack of food and supplies. At the end of the war, Davis was arrested on the charge of treason and spent two years in prison. Although he was pardoned, he was denied U.S. citizenship for the rest of his life.

John Brown and the Fight against Slavery
(Gateway Civil Rights Series)
Written by James L. Collins
Illustrated with black-and-white and color photographs and prints
Millbrook Press, 1991
32 pages, chronology, bibliography, index
　　Major events in Brown's life, including his childhood with parents who hated slavery, his two marriages and 20 children, his obsession with eliminating slavery, the battle at Harper's Ferry, and his death by execution, are described. Other abolitionists, such as Harriet Tubman, Harriet Beecher Stowe, and Henry Ward Beecher, and some history of the movement, including some of the major compromises and the Dred Scot case, are included.

Lincoln: A Photobiography
Written by Russell Freedman
Illustrated with black-and-white photographs
Clarion, 1987
150 pages, bibliography, index
　　Lincoln comes to life through Freedman's technique of showing readers what is important rather than telling them. The interesting details and carefully chosen photographs provide an engrossing story of this complex man. Incidents from throughout Lincoln's life, beginning with his boyhood and including the victories and defeats of his adult life, provide insights into the decisions he made and the kind of person he was.

Robert E. Lee
Written by Nathan Aaseng
Lerner Publications Company, 1991
112 pages, maps, bibliography, index
　　As the last of the classic generals, Lee led the Confederate army gallantly in a struggle he knew was doomed from the start. In his youth and throughout his training at West Point, Lee was constantly hampered by the irresponsible behaviors of his father and older brother. His career in the peacetime Union army was boring

and unrewarding. He distinguished himself during the Mexican War, but continued to serve in low-ranking positions until the onset of the Civil War. President Lincoln offered him the position of field commander of the Union army, but Lee decided his loyalty lay with his home state of Virginia. Rejecting both slavery and secession, he fought to defend his home and family.

Robert E. Lee
Written by Manfred Weidhorn
Illustrated with black-and-white photographs
Atheneum, 1988
150 pages, bibliography, index

A true southern gentleman, Robert E. Lee maintained his alliance to his home state of Virginia throughout his life. He turned down Lincoln's offer to be field commander of the Union army, hoping that Virginia would remain neutral and he could avoid the war. In his leadership role, he was more likely to make suggestions than give orders, and he suffered defeats due to incompetent officers under his command. His troops loved him, and his strategic maneuvers enabled him to keep fighting much longer than would have been predicted, given his limited number of soldiers and scarcity of supplies. His last days were spent productively as president of Washington and Lee College.

Sojourner Truth
(Black Americans of Achievement Series)
Written by Peter Krass
Illustrated with black-and-white photographs and prints
Chelsea House Publishers, 1988
110 pages, chronology, bibliography, index

Sojourner Truth was born a slave (named Isabella) in New York in 1797. She had five owners before she was officially freed from slavery in 1827. She could not read or write, but dictated the story of her life to a friend, and it was published as The Narrative of Sojourner Truth. She traveled extensively throughout the North, lecturing for abolitionist and women's suffrage causes. In later years she had official meetings with both President Lincoln and President Grant.

Stonewall
Written by Jean Fritz
Illustrated by Stephen Gammell
G. P. Putnam's Sons, 1979
155 pages, bibliography

Thomas Jackson was a deeply religious man who expected high moral conduct from himself and those around him. His life was conducted according to rules and regulations, many of which he imposed on himself. His rigid behavior caused him to clash with other officers in his first military assignments after graduating from West Point, and it generated unpopularity among his students at the Virginia Military Institute. He was disappointed that the Mexican War ended too quickly for him to become a hero, so he was pleased to have another opportunity when the Civil War began. He inspired his troops with his bravery, his military strategies, and steadfastness in battle. When he died from complications of battle injuries two years before the war ended, he was given a hero's funeral in both Richmond and Lexington. His legend continued as Confederate soldiers recounted his many brave actions and his interesting idiosyncrasies throughout the rest of the war and thereafter.

Ulysses S. Grant: Eighteenth President of the United States
(Encyclopedia of Presidents)
Written by Zachary Kent
Illustrated with black-and-white photographs and prints
Children's Press, 1989
100 pages, index

Grant's story begins with the Battle of Shiloh and then flashes back to his childhood. After an undistinguished stint at West Point, he began his military career in St. Louis, Missouri. He was recognized for this brave and faithful service during the Mexican War and was then stationed in an outpost in Michigan before being sent to the Pacific coast. He drank to blot out loneliness and boredom, which caused his resignation from the army. When war broke out he was given command of an Illinois volunteer regiment. He was involved in a number of battles and was asked by President Lincoln to command the Union army in the field in 1864. He was, therefore, the general that accepted Robert E. Lee's surrender of the Confederate army. He served as president of the United States from

1869–1877. A chronology of U.S. history, with the years of Grant's lifetime highlighted, is included.

William Tecumseh Sherman: Champion of the Union
Written by Charles P. Graves
Illustrated by Pers Crowell
Garrard Publishing Company, 1986
112 pages, index

Left fatherless as a young child, Sherman was raised by kind neighbors and chose to go to West Point so he could receive a free education. He saw no action during the Mexican War, remaining in a California outpost station and advancing through the military ranks slowly. Although he was later stationed in Louisiana and had many friends in the South, he immediately made himself available for the Union army at the start of the war. He was placed in charge of five regiments and was soon promoted to brigadier general. An account of the battles he led and his march through Georgia are described. After the war Sherman negotiated treaties with the western Indians and was appointed commanding general of the armies of the United States by President Grant. Sherman is credited with having coined the remark, War is hell.

Fiction Books

Across Five Aprils
Written by Irene Hunt
Follet Publishing Company, 1964
190 pages

Set in southern Illinois, Jethro's story begins in April 1861 and continues through April 1865. At first he shares the excitement of his older brothers about the impending war, but he soon discovers that war does not bring the anticipated adventure and glory. The agony of the war is dramatically portrayed as his beloved brother chooses to fight for the South while his other brothers join forces with the North. An account of the war's major battles is incorporated into the story through reports of newspaper articles and excerpts from letters sent from the front. The news of Lincoln's death convinces Jethro that peace is not the perfect pearl he had expected.

Be Ever Hopeful, Hannalee
Written by Patricia Beatty
Morrow Junior Books, 1988
216 pages

This sequel to Turn Homeward, Hannalee takes place in Atlanta after the end of the war. Hannalee's family moves into a refugee camp on the edge of town, and each family member finds work to provide food and earn money for moving to a better place. Davey, Hannalee's older brother, lost an arm in the war and cannot return to his trade as a carpenter. The devastation of Atlanta and the effects on all people as they attempt to rebuild the city and their lives provides a clear sense of the war's aftermath.

Charley Skedaddle
Written by Patricia Beatty
Morrow Junior Books, 1987
186 pages

A street-wise, New York 12-year-old sneaks aboard a troop ship headed for Virginia to avenge the death of his beloved older brother who died at Gettysburg. He enlists as a drummer boy, but realizes the war is not as glamorous as he expected when he sees his first battle. He runs to the hills and eventually finds courage in another setting, proving to himself that he is not a coward, after all.

Eben Tyne, Powdermonkey
Written by Patricia Beatty and Phillip Robbins
Morrow Junior Books, 1990
227 pages

Living in Norfork, Virginia, during the Union blockade of the harbor, 13-year-old Eben Tyne finds his life changed as his strength and courage are challenged. Having demonstrated his capabilities helping the South, he is selected to serve on the famous ironclad, Merrimack, as a powder carrier. Struggling with loyalties to his mother and friends, he experiences the danger and excitement of the ship's battles against Union vessels, including the famous *Monitor*.

Listen for Rachel
Written by Lou Kassem
Margaret K. McElderry Books, 1986
165 pages

Rachel finds her true calling in life when she goes to live with her grandparents in the Appalachian Mountains of Tennessee following the death of her parents. She comes to love the mountain people and is chosen by Granny Sharp to learn the ways of medicine and healing. When the war breaks out, Rachel's grandfather declares his land to be neutral as his two sons and their families choose different allegiances. When a wounded young Yankee officer wanders onto their land, Rachel falls in love with him as she nurses him back to health. He returns to marry Rachel after the war and she becomes the legendary healer on whom the story is based.

Rifles for Watie
Written by Harold Keith
Thomas Y. Crowell, 1957
332 pages

Expecting to participate in the glamor of war, 16-year-old Jeff Bussey left his Kansas home and signed on with the Union forces. He was sadly disappointed when he discovered that the war was mostly long marches and constant hunger. The battles were terrifying, and losing comrades was heart-wrenching. Meeting some rebel families and fraternizing with rebel troops along the way convinces him that the enemy is not so bad. In fact, after serving as a spy behind enemy lines for a time, he's not sure where his loyalties lie.

The Root Cellar
Written by Janet Lunn
Charles Scribner's Sons, 1981
229 pages

This time-shift story offers a Canadian viewpoint of the war. At first, Rose, an unhappy orphan sent to live with relatives in Canada, is delighted to find her way back into the 1860s, where she befriends Susan, a young servant girl and Will, Susan's boyfriend. Then Will decides to cross the border with his American cousin and join the Union army. When Will does not return, Rose convinces Susan they must go find him. The girls travel alone from Hawthorne Bay, Canada, to Washington, D.C., where they find Will at Arlington Cemetery grieving the loss of his cousin. Will is seriously ill as a result of injuries suffered in the campaign on Richmond.

The Sacred Moon Tree:
Being a True Account of the Trials and Adventures
of Phoebe Sands in the Great War between the States, 1861–1865
Written by Laura Jan Shore
Bradbury Press, 1986
209 pages

An imaginative 12-year-old girl talks a neighbor boy into traveling from Pennsylvania (near Philadelphia) to Richmond, Virginia, to rescue his brother from a Confederate prison. They become involved with the war on both sides. Graphic descriptions of battles and wounded soldiers convey the tragedy of war. In the course of achieving her purpose, Phoebe discovers her father has lost a leg fighting in the Union army and her mother has been serving as a spy for the Union cause.

Shades of Gray
Written by Carolyn Reeder
Macmillan Publishing Company, 1989
152 pages

The lingering aftermath of the war is realistically portrayed in this story of Will Page, who is sent to live with relatives in the Virginia Piedmont after his father is killed while fighting as a Confederate soldier, and the other members of his family have died of causes attributable to the war. Will is resentful toward his uncle who chose not to join either army. To make matters even worse, his uncle takes in a Yankee soldier in need of rest on his way home! This seems more than an angry young man can handle. Will grudgingly comes to love and respect his uncle as he learns about true courage.

The Slopes of War
Written by N. A. Perez
Houghton Mifflin Company, 1984
202 pages

Living in Gettysburg, Pennsylvania, in July 1863, Beckah Summerfield is placed in the heart of the battles that took place there.

While her allegiance is to the North, she has friends and relatives with the armies of both sides. She is torn between conflicts of loyalty and fear as she attempts to assist the injured and dying. An accurate portrayal is presented of the Battle of Gettysburg and the sorrow that followed. President Lincoln's famous address at the dedication of the cemetery contributes to the emotional impact.

Turn Homeward, Hannalee
Written by Patricia Beatty
William Morrow and Company, 1984
193 pages

In July 1864 the Yankee cavalry rounded up textile workers from three mill towns in Georgia, declared them to be traitors because they were making supplies for the Confederate army, and transported them to Tennessee and Kentucky. Beatty has based her story in this historical incident. Her spunky, 12-year-old heroine saves the meager wages she earns, finds her younger brother, and manages to get both of them safely back to Georgia. The tragedy of the war is expressed from a variety of viewpoints.

Uncle Tom's Cabin
Written by Harriet Beecher Stowe
Original copyright, 1852
Available in a variety of reprints

This classic story of slavery presents a broad view of both slaves and masters. Uncle Tom is presented as the long-suffering slave who accepted his lot in life without complaint and practiced Christian virtue in spite of all hardships. He was rewarded for his steadfastness by being beaten to death by a harsh owner. Other slaves fare better. Daring escapes prove successful and some families are reunited. The sorrow of separation from family is an underlying current throughout the story. Mature readers will find this a fascinating account of this historical period.

Underground Man
Written by Milton Meltzer
Harcourt Brace Jovanovich, 1990
261 pages

Based on the life of Calvin Franklin, the fictional Joshua Bowen is an abolitionist who went into the South to rescue slaves and help

them to freedom in the North. After participating in many successful rescues, Josh was arrested and found guilty. The deplorable
conditions of prison existence are graphically described. When he
was released after serving five years, he traveled the lecture circuit
for a time, speaking on abolitionist issues. Then he resumed his
rescue efforts and was returned to prison, where he remained until
the beginning of the Civil War.

Which Way Freedom

(Walker's American History Series for Young People)
Written by Joyce Hansen
Walker and Company, 1986
120 pages

Using a flashback technique, this story introduces Obi, an
escaped slave, who is serving in the Union Army. The scene then
shifts to Obi's early memories of his mother crying as he was
wrenched from her and sold separately. His life as a slave on a
relatively small farm is described. When he is hired out to work on
a large plantation nearby, he is captured with a group of slaves and
forced to labor for the Confederate Army. He helps several others
weave a boat from grass and escapes with one other man. The story
then returns to the opening setting just as the massacre at Fort
Pillow, Tennessee, is beginning. Obi survives by acting dead and
manages to rescue his friend. Black dialect is used for conversations
and each chapter is introduced with a quotation from writings of
the time.

Zoar Blue

Written by Janet Hickman
Macmillan Publishing Company, Inc., 1978
140 pages

The extent of the impact of the war is revealed in this story set
in Zoar, Ohio. Two young people from this isolated German Sepa-
ratist community are featured. Gentle seventeen-year-old John
Keffer joins the Union Army in spite of the pacifist policy of the
Society, and a thirteen-year-old orphan, Barbara Hoff, leaves to
find relatives of her own. John is unprepared for the reality of war.
He witnesses the death of several of his friends and barely survives
himself, returning home with a wounded arm and typhoid. Barbara finds her uncle's place, but not her uncle, and returns to Zoar

after helping to nurse survivors of Gettysburg. Shifting viewpoints allow the reader to experience the effects of the war from a variety of perspectives.

Sample Lesson Plan

Introduction

Read *Cecil's Story* by George Ella Lyon aloud to the class. What does this story reveal about the Civil War? Discuss what students know about this war. How was it different from other wars the United States has been involved in? Use a map of the United States to point out the Union states, the Confederate states, the border states, and the territories in 1861. Note the position of the state you are living in.

Building Background

Meet in the school library. Ask each student to work with a partner to find as many causes for the Civil War as possible. They may look for information in library books, computer programs, encyclopedias, and other reference materials. Instruction in using these sources and in appropriate ways to record information may be led by the librarian or the classroom teacher.

Conduct a class discussion on the causes of the Civil War. Ask students if they can identify large categories for the major causes. List these on separate pieces of chart paper or transparencies. Three of the categories most likely to surface are economic differences, states' rights, and slavery. Then list individual causes on the appropriate chart paper or transparency. Keep the lists for future reference.

Beginning Preparations for a Class Newspaper

Preparing a special edition of a newspaper to report on the Civil War can provide an ongoing method of organizing and summarizing information as the unit progress. Students may begin the process by studying daily and weekly newspapers. What are their names? Why were these names chosen? What are the formats? What types of columns and features are included in each? Is there a consistent pattern of organization from issue to issue?

Invite the editor of one of the local newspapers to speak to the class. Prepare a list of questions prior to the visit. Some questions might be: Who decides which news events will be headlined? How much space is normally allotted to specific types of stories? Who determines editorial policy? What qualifications do local and syndicated columnists generally have?

Begin a discussion of the class newspaper, including possibilities for a good name. Applications can be developed and distributed for jobs such as managing editor, layout editor, obituary editor, reporters, columnists, reviewers of books and other media, and political cartoonists. If assignments of duties are made near the beginning of the unit of study, students will have time to produce high-quality contributions.

Issues

Slavery

Read *Nettie's Trip South* by Ann Turner aloud to the class. Discuss the issue of slavery in the historical perspective of the time. Why did slavery become so prominent in the South while it almost ceased to exist in the North? Read a chapter or two from *Escape from Slavery* by Doreen Rappaport aloud to the class. What do these accounts tell us about the attitude of slaves toward their bondage?

Meet in the school library. Brainstorm possible solutions to the slavery issue as it stood in 1860. Assign students topics to research relating to the issue and attempts to solve it. Suggested topics include: the Missouri Compromise, the Compromise of 1850, the Kansas-Nebraska Act, the Anthony Burns Case, the Dred Scott Case, and John Brown's raid on Harper's Ferry.

Set up a mock U.S. Senate. Appoint a chairperson, a parliamentarian and a recorder. (Talk to the students about their roles a few days before the session so they will be ready to play them effectively.) Divide the rest of the students into two groups, one representing senators from the Northern states and the other representing senators from the Southern states. Reenact a debate that could have occurred in the Senate in 1860 as that body tried to resolve the slavery issue.

Some students may serve as reporters covering the event for the class newspaper.

Secession of the Southern States

Discuss the secession of the Southern states and the formation of the Confederate government. What were the reasons for seceding? Why was Jefferson Davis selected as president? Read Chapter 1 from *A Nation Torn: The Story of How the Civil War Began* by Delia Ray to the class.

Major Battles and Turning Points

Was war inevitable before the firing on Fort Sumter? After the firing? Why was the lack of casualties at Fort Sumter misleading in predicting the battles to come?

Some other topics for discussion include the Siege of Vicksburg, the Battle of Chattanooga, Sherman's march through Georgia, and the meeting of Generals Grant and Lee at Appomattox.

The Battle of Gettysburg

Read aloud *Thunder at Gettysburg* by Patricia Lee Gauch. Discuss the Battle of Gettysburg and why it is considered to be the turning point of the war. Read Lincoln's Gettysburg Address aloud. How was it received at the time it was delivered?

Political and Military Leadership

Discuss the prominent people of the time. Why did the choice of generals to lead the forces cause problems for both sides?

Abraham Lincoln

Read the first chapter of *Lincoln: A Photobiography* by Russell Freedman aloud to the class. Make a list of "facts" students know about Lincoln on chart paper or transparencies. Make another list of questions they are curious about. Ask students to find out as much about Lincoln as they can. Multiple paperback copies of the Freedman book may be available in the classroom. Students may also go to the school library to find other biographies and to use reference materials. An outline for notetaking can be provided. Suggested topics are Lincoln's boyhood, education, law practice, marriage and family, politics, debates with Stephen Douglas, 1860 presidential campaign, presidency, and death.

Divide students into groups of three or four to discuss Abraham Lincoln. Ask the recorder in each group to list the five most interesting facts discovered about Lincoln. Share these facts with the whole group and then review the "facts" and questions recorded earlier. Which "facts" proved correct and which incorrect? Were all of the questions answered? Ask students to write a eulogy (not to exceed 300 words) that would have been appropriate to print in a newspaper following Lincoln's death. Some representative pieces may be chosen for the class newspaper.

Other Leaders

Meet in the school library. Briefly discuss the roles of leaders, other than Lincoln, in the Civil War. Divide the students into groups of three or four. Ask each group to find as much information as possible about a particular military or political leader. Suggested leaders include Jefferson Davis, Robert E. Lee, Ulysses Grant, Stonewall Jackson, William T. Sherman, Pierre G.T. Beauregard, Philip H. Sheridan, James E. B. Stuart, George B. McClellan, Stand Watie, David G. Farragut, Leonidas Polk, and Andrew Foote.

Ask each group to write a eulogy of the assigned person for the class newspaper.

Compare notes on leaders. Which ones were most effective. What types of mistakes were made? What would have been the effect on the war if Robert E. Lee had agreed to serve as field commander of the Union Army when asked by Abraham Lincoln?

Projects

Distribute a list of recommended projects for the Civil War. This list can be compiled from suggested activities included with this unit and general activities recommended in the introduction. Students may have the option of designing their own projects with the approval of the teacher or the school librarian. Allow time for students to look for resources and think about their choice of a project. They may work in the classroom or school library as appropriate.

A display of projects may be presented during a class session. Class reporters may cover this presentation for the newspaper.

Fiction Books

Using well-written fiction books can add a dimension to the study that would be missing if only factual materials were used.

Across Five Aprils by Irene Hunt is recommended as a good example of the use of fiction to provide a personalized understanding of the effects of the war on people at home.

Distribute paperback copies of *Across Five Aprils* to students. Ask students to read the book, keeping literary qualities and the experience of the Civil War in mind. A study guide may be distributed to assist students in thinking about the significance of the story.

Study Guide for **Across Five Aprils**

- **Setting.** How does the setting in southern Illinois provide an appropriate framework for this particular story? Would this have been a different story if Jethro had lived in Maine or in Georgia? In what ways?
- **Main Character.** Jethro grows from the age of 9 to 14 in this story. How does this age span add authenticity to the story? Which characters are most influential in Jethro's life? In what ways? How does the phrase "a boy in time of peace and a man in time of war" apply to Jethro?
- **Point of View.** How is the reader's view of the war expanded through learning about it from Jethro's viewpoint? How is it restricted? How would the story be different if the author had included other viewpoints, such as those of Ellen, Matt, Bill, or Shadrach?
- **Plot.** How does the author incorporate major events of the war into the story? How does using the month of April contribute to the plot structure?
- **Author's Style of Writing.** Why do you think the author chose to use dialect for conversations among the people of southern Illinois?
- **Theme.** State what the book is really about in one sentence.

Discuss *Across Five Aprils* in terms of literary qualities. How does this story contribute to a deeper understanding of the war? Ask students who read additional books to share insights they have gained.

Other Fiction Books

Students may choose to read other fiction books which present viewpoints of both the North and the South. The reporting form for fiction books in Appendix B may be used to respond to the books. Some students may choose to write reviews to submit to the class newspaper.

Effects of the War

Read aloud several selections from Milton Meltzer's *Voices from the Civil War*. Ask students to choose one person or category of person for research. Suggested categories are a Confederate Soldier; a Union Soldier; a civilian woman in the North or South; a child in the North or South; a free black man, woman, or child; or a slave. Ask students to write a diary for one week that could have been kept by one of these people reflecting both daily life and how the war was affecting that person. Select excerpts from some of the journals for inclusion in the class newspaper.

Place students in two groups according to types of categories selected, one group reflecting the Southern experience and one the Northern. The classroom teacher can direct the discussion for one group and the school librarian can lead the other. Meet together part way through the session to share experiences.

Culminating Activity

Ask students to write an editorial about the conclusion of the war and the effects on the people from either the Northern or Southern viewpoint. Choose several of the best for each perspective for the class newspaper.

Complete the organization and publication of the class newspaper on the Civil War. Reports based on all class activities and pieces of writing from throughout the unit may be included.

The publication may be distributed to students and parents in the school, to school and district administrators, and to teachers of the Civil War in other schools and districts.

Suggested Questions

How was it possible that large numbers of boys between the ages of 12 and 17 from both sides fought in many major battles when recruitment rules specified 18 as the youngest age for enlistment?

When slavery was first introduced to the colonies in 1619, it was not restricted to any particular area. How did slavery become so

When slavery was first introduced to the colonies in 1619, it was not restricted to any particular area. How did slavery become so prominent in the South while it became almost nonexistent in the North?

Why were both free and slave states so concerned about the slavery status for new states as they entered the Union?

What was the purpose of the Missouri Compromise, and how successful was it?

How did the application of Kansas to become a state escalate violence over the slavery issue?

Why did the Dred Scott case cause intense anger among abolitionists?

What was the significance of the book Uncle Tom's Cabin by Harriet Beecher Stowe?

What were the major issues in the presidential campaign of 1860?

What was Abraham Lincoln's position on the slavery issue prior to his election to the presidency?

How might the war have progressed differently if Robert E. Lee had accepted President Lincoln's offer to become the field commander for the Union forces?

Why did General Lee decide to join with the Confederate cause instead of the Union cause?

What reasons did most of the common soldiers have for joining their respective armies?

What were living conditions like for most of the soldiers?

How would the war have been affected if foreign countries, such as Great Britain or France, had joined forces with the Confederacy?

What were the causes of the draft riots in New York City?

Why was the Battle of Gettysburg considered to be the turning point of the war?

How was Lincoln's Gettysburg Address received at the time it was delivered?

What was the reaction throughout the country to Abraham Lincoln's Emancipation Proclamation?

Why is the Civil War considered to be one of the saddest chapters in United States history?

How would the history of the United States and the present condition of the country (or countries) have been different if the Confederacy had won the war?

Suggested Activities

Construct a chart showing powers that are reserved for the states and powers that are granted to the federal government according to the Constitution of the United States. Have these powers changed between 1860 and the present time?

Make a chart contrasting the ideals and values of the South with those of the North in 1860.

Construct a chart contrasting the economic basis of the Northern and Southern states prior to 1860.

Make a graph showing the percentages of families who owned slaves in each of the Southern states in 1861. Break this down to show families that owned fewer than 5 slaves, between 5 and 100 slaves, and over 100 slaves.

Read *Uncle Tom's Cabin* by Harriet Beecher Stowe and explain how it contributed to the increasing animosity between free and slave states.

Write a journal that could have been kept by Dred Scott from the time he left his owners through the decision of his case by the Supreme Court.

Dramatize an incident between battles when Confederate and Union soldiers fraternized with each other.

Paint a mural of the Battle of Gettysburg.

Construct a graph comparing the numbers of deaths due to battles, disease, and imprisonment. Accompany this with descriptions of hospitals, medical procedures, and prisons.

Construct a chart depicting the contribution of black people to the war effort.

Construct a diorama of the battle of the Virginia (Merrimack) and the Monitor.

Reenact General Lee's surrender to General Grant at Appomattox.

Reenact the Lincoln-Douglas debates.

Write an article that could have appeared in a newspaper following Abraham Lincoln's election to the presidency.

Make a list and briefly describe the economic acts passed by Congress during Lincoln's presidency that contributed to the United States becoming a great industrial power.

Create a booklet of sayings attributed to Abraham Lincoln.

Read a biography of one of the influential people of the era and prepare a script for an interview with the person.

Create a songbook of songs that originated during the Civil War.

Glossary

abolitionist—A person opposed to slavery in the United States.

assassination—The murder of a politically prominent person.

Billy Yank—Nickname for a Union soldier.

bushwhackers—People in Kansas Territory who favored entering the Union as a free state.

compromise—A settlement of differences in which each side gives up some demands or makes some sacrifices in order to reach an agreement.

Compromise of 1850—A series of acts passed by Congress that prohibited slave trade in Washington, D.C., admitted California to the Union as a free state, allowed newly acquired territories to decide the slavery issue for themselves, and allowed for the return of fugitive slaves to their masters.

Confederate States of America—The alliance of 11 southern states that withdrew from the United States in 1860 and 1861. These states were Alabama, Arkansas, Florida, Georgia, Louisiana, Mississippi, North Carolina, South Carolina, Tennessee, Texas, and Virginia.

conscientious objector—A person whose religious or personal beliefs prevent him from fighting in wars.

cotton diplomacy—Efforts of Confederate statesmen to use the foreign appetite for southern cotton to persuade European powers to help the Confederacy's war effort.

cotton gin—A machine invented by Eli Whitney in 1793 that removed the hard seeds from cotton fibers, thereby making cotton a profitable crop and contributing to the expansion of slavery.

delegate—A person chosen to represent a certain group in decision making.

Democratic party—A political organization that believed in the rights of the states over the rights of the federal government.

dog tags—Identification, usually name and address, written on a handkerchief or paper and pinned to a soldier's uniform prior to battle.

draft riots—Crowds in New York City in 1863 protested the draft law that allowed men to pay $300 to avoid going into the army.

Dred Scott decision—A Supreme Court decision denying Dred Scott's claim to freedom and declaring that no black could be a citizen of the United States.

Emancipation Proclamation—A statement issued by Abraham Lincoln declaring that all slaves held in states rebelling against the United States were then and from that day forward free.

federal—Associated with the national government based in Washington, D.C.

foraging—Living off the land by hunting wild animals, gathering berries and nuts, and extracting honey from beehives.

Fourteenth Amendment—Declares that all persons born or naturalized in the United States are citizens entitled to full rights and privileges and to equal protection of the law.

fraternization—Associating with enemy soldiers.

fugitive—A person who flees; a runaway.

garrisonA fort or military post and the troops stationed there.

Gettysburg—A town in Pennsylvania where a major battle occurred, causing the greatest loss of life in any three-day period during the Civil War.

Gettysburg Address—Abraham Lincoln's brief, eloquent dedication of the Gettysburg Cemetery.

Great Emancipator—A term used to refer to Abraham Lincoln for his role in freeing the slaves.

habeas corpus—The right of a person under arrest to be heard in court.

hardtack—Hard biscuits eaten by the soldiers.

Harper's Ferry (raid)—An unsuccessful attempt by John Brown and other abolitionists to start a slave rebellion.

Impressment Act of 1863—Permitted Confederate government agents to seize food, horses, and supplies from civilians for army use.

ironclad—Wooden ship covered with iron plates.

jayhawkers—Antislavery guerillas in Kansas and Missouri before and during the Civil War.

Kansas-Nebraska Act—Made slavery possible in territories where it had been prohibited by the Missouri Compromise; left the decision to a popular vote at the time of application for statehood.

Know-Nothing party—A political party in existence from 1854 to 1860 that blamed immigrants and Roman Catholics for the country's problems.

legislature—A group of people invested with the power to make laws for a country or a state.

liberation—The act of becoming free or granting freedom.

mass grave—Trenches in which unidentified corpses are buried after a battle.

Missouri Compromise—Prohibited slavery in territories north of an imaginary line extending west from Missouri's southern border.

overseer—A person who supervises the work of others; one who supervised the work of slaves on southern plantations.

pacifist—A person opposed to using war or violence in settling disputes.

parapet—A low wall along the edge of a fort's roof designed to protect soldiers from enemy fire.

plantation—A large agricultural estate where crops were tended by slaves.

popular sovereignty—A policy that allowed territories applying for statehood to decide by popular vote whether to be free or slave.

racism—A belief that racial differences produce an inherent superiority of a particular race.

rebel—Term used for a supporter of the Confederacy.

rebel yell—A loud war whoop hollered by Confederate soldiers as they went into battle.

Reconstruction—The reorganization and reintegration of the seceded states into the Union after the war.

Republican party—A major political party organized in the United States in the 1850s on the basis of opposition to the spread of slavery.

secession—The withdrawal of membership from an organization or of states from the federal union.

shoddy—Rewoven wool that fell apart easily; used for many uniforms.

states' rights—Belief in the authority of state government over federal government.

sutler—A peddler who followed the troops, selling food and other supplies for highly inflated prices.

Thirteenth Amendment—An amendment to the Constitution of the United States abolishing slavery.

Underground Railroad—A system established by abolitionists to help fugitive slaves escape from the South to free states or Canada.

Union—Term commonly used for the United States during the Civil War.

volunteer—A person who enlists in either army of his own free will.

white supremacy—The belief that people of the white races are inherently superior to those of other races.

Yankee—Term used for a Northerner.

World War I Literature Unit

Selected Chronology

1879		Germany and Austria-Hungary formed an alliance.
1882		Triple Alliance formed when Italy joined with Germany and Austria-Hungary.
1894		France and Russia formed the Dual Alliance.
1904		Great Britain and France formed *Entente Cordiale* (an informal agreement rather than a rigid alliance).
1905		Germany's war plan prepared by Alfred von Schlieffen, chief of the German General Staff.
1914	June 28	Assassination of Archduke Franz Ferdinand.
	July 30	Russia began to mobilize its military forces.
	August 1	Germany declared war on Russia.
	August 3	Germany declared war on France.
	August 4	Germany invaded Belgium.
	August 4	Great Britain declared war on Germany.
	August	Japan declared war on Germany.
	September 6	First Battle of the Marne.
	November	The Allies declared war on the Ottoman Empire.
1915	April 22	Germans used poisonous gases in warfare for the first time during the Battle of Ypres.
	May 7	The sinking of the *Lusitania* by the Germans aroused American anger against Germany.
	May 23	Italy joined the war on the side of the Allied Forces.
	June 3	The Turkish government killed 1.5 million Armenians suspected of supporting the Russians.
	June–July	Russia lost Galicia, Lithuania, and Poland to Germany and Austria-Hungary.
1916	February	Battle of Verdun.
	May 31	Naval battle of Jutland.
	August 29	Rumania entered the war on the Allied side.
	November 24	Greece entered the war against Bulgaria and Germany.

	December	Germany proposed peace to the Allies with the United States acting as an intermediary, but the Allies refused.
1917	March	Russian Revolution forced Czar Nicholas II from the throne.
	April 6	The United States entered the war on the side of the Allies.
	May	The mutiny in the French army was solved by Commander in Chief Petain.
	November	Lenin and the Bolsheviks seized power of the Russian government and moved to end Russian involvement in the war.
1918	March 3	Treaty of Brest-Litovsk between Soviet Union and Germany ended war in the East.
	July–August	Second Battle of the Marne.
	November 9	Kaiser Wilhelm II abdicated, and the socialist Schneidemann proclaimed a republic in Germany.
	November 11	Germany accepted the terms of armistice of the Allies and the war was over.
1919	January	Paris Peace Conference began with representatives of Allied nations. Losing nations were not represented.
	June 28	Treaty of Paris signed at the Palace of Versailles.
	September 10	The Treaty of Saint Germain-en-Laye reduced Austria-Hungary to just Austria and established the independent nations of Czechoslovakia, Hungary, Poland, and Yugoslavia.

Recommended Books

Picture Books

World War I
(Silver Burdett Picture Histories Series)
Written by Pierre Miquel
Translated from the French by Charlotte M. Kossmann
Illustrated by Jacques Poirier
Silver Burdett, 1985
63 pages, chronology, glossary, index

A concisely worded text and full color illustrations provide basic information in an interesting format. Each two-page spread features a half-page illustration and half a page of text faced by a full page of smaller pictures with explanatory text for each. The 24 topics include the war's effects on civilians and refugees as well as accounts of major types of warfare. A Diary of the War at the conclusion provides a chronology of major events, mentioning some of the significant people of the time.

World War I
(Wars that Changed the World Series)
Written by Ken Hills
Illustrated by W. Francis Phillips
Marshall Cavendish, 1988
32 pages, maps, index

Each double-page spread features a topic about the war accompanied by extensive full-color illustrations. The account begins with the assassination of Archduke Franz Ferdinand. Types of warfare and major battles are described. It concludes with a chapter entitled Illusion of Victory. A list of important events and people is included.

Factual Books

An Album of World War I
Written by Dorothy Hoobler and Thomas Hoobler
Illustrated with black-and-white photographs
Franklin Watts, 1976
96 pages, maps, index

An accessible account of the war, beginning with a description of Europe before the war and an explanation of the major causes of the war. A chapter for each year (19141918) presents significant events and battles in various parts of the world. The closing epilogue discusses the Versailles Conference, the Peace Treaty, and the enduring effects of the war.

The Attack on the *Lusitania*
(Great Disasters Series)
Written by Rupert Matthews
Illustrated by Nik Spender
The Bookwright Press, 1989
32 pages, glossary, bibliography, index

This account of the German sinking of a passenger ship en route from New York to Liverpool begins with a survivor's description of the explosion, evacuation, and rescue. This is followed by a brief explanation of the war to that point and a further discussion of the attack and rescue efforts. A cutaway view of the *Lusitania* shows the luxurious liner's impressive layout. The significance of the incident in affecting public opinion in the United States and throughout the world is described as the angry aftermath.

The Trenches: Fighting on the Western Front in World War I
Written by Dorothy and Thomas Hoobler
Illustrated with black and white photographs
G. P. Putnam's Sons, 1978
191 pages, bibliography, index

This Great War of 1914–1918 marked the end of the age of innocence. The advances in weaponry and the destruction caused by modern warfare effectively eliminated the romanticism of war. The development of large military organizations directed from headquarters remote from the battlefield is described. Trenches, which began as temporary foxholes, soon became permanent fixtures cutting across the face of Europe. Allied and German structures were protected by barbed wire and separated by a narrow strip of "no man's land." Miserable living conditions and exchanges of fire resulted in the futile loss of many lives. Those who survived suffered such long-lasting effects that they became known as "the lost generation."

The Versailles Treaty, 1919:
Germany's Formal Surrender at the End of the Great War
(World Focus Book Series)
Written by Harold Cecil Vaughn
Illustrated with black-and-white pictures
Franklin Watts, 1975
66 pages, bibliography, index

Presenting a well-written summary of the peace conference and the terms of the treaty, this book is a good resource for research. The Big Four leaders are described with brief biographical information and their preconceived goals for the conference. Each aspect of the treaty is carefully explained and then the German response is given. A conclusion places the document in historical perspective.

World War I
(A First Book Series)
Written by Louis L. Snyder
Illustrated with black-and-white photographs
Franklin Watts, 1981. Revised edition
90 pages, maps, glossary, index

This book provides a comprehensible presentation of the war. Major battles and events throughout the world are explained. The clearly formatted account begins with the murder at Sarajevo. It discusses various types of war activities, such as bombings, land battles, and conflicts at sea and in the air. The cost of the war and its far-reaching results provide a fitting conclusion.

World War One: An Illustrated History in Colour, 1914–1918
Written by Robert Hoare
Edited by R. J. Unstead
Special advisor: Dr. J. M. Roberts
McDonald Educational, [1973] 1979. Fourth reprint
64 pages, maps, graphs, bibliography, index

Profusely illustrated with both full-color and black-and-white illustrations, the 30 topics in this book cover the major events of the war and the types of warfare waged. A section of poems and songs provides a perspective on the lives and fears of common soldiers.

World War I Battleship
(Fighting Ships Series)
Written by Richard Humble
Illustrated by Doug Harker
Franklin Watts, 1989
32 pages, glossary, time chart, index

This book contains a detailed description of the dreadnought battleships, including the training and living conditions of the crews who served on them. A comprehensive description of the Battle of Jutland is clearly illustrated with full-color drawings and black-and-white photographs.

The World War I Tommy
(The Soldier through the Ages Series)
Written by Martin Windrow
Illustrated by Richard Hook
Franklin Watts, 1986
32 pages, chronology, glossary, index

This colorfully illustrated book provides a detailed description of the uniform and equipment of the British soldier. The construction of the trench system and the soldiers' miserable living conditions are vividly described. The horrors of no-man's-land and the futility of battle in a war locked in stalemate contributed to the deep sense of frustration felt by the troops at the front.

Biographies

Bold Leaders of World War I
Written by Colonel Red Reeder
Illustrated with black-and-white photographs
Little, Brown and Company, 1974
252 pages, maps, bibliography, index

Concise biographies averaging about 13 to 15 pages summarize the major contributions of 12 people during the war. People from both sides of the war are represented, some famous and some little known. Those included are Erich Ludendorff, General Joffre, Edith Cavell, Fritz Kreisler, Winston Churchill, Philippe Petain, Bill Brekinridge, Carl Mannerheim, Manfred von Richthofen, Laurence Stallings, George C. Marshall, and Ralph Eaton. The introductory chapter discusses the differences between World War I and World War II.

Flying Aces of World War I
Written by Gene Gurney
Illustrated with black-and-white photographs
Random House, 1965
185 pages, bibliography, index

The first chapter explains the use of airplanes in World War I. The remaining chapters are each devoted to an ace. Included are Georges Guynemer, Albert Ball, Manfred von Richthofen, Raoul Lufbry, Edward Mannock, Willy Coppens, Dave Ingalls, and Eddie Rickenbacker. A list of major aces from each country and their numbers of scores concludes the book.

Illustrious Americans: John J. Pershing
Written by Frank E. Vandiver and the editors of Silver Burdett (editor in
*   charge: Sam Welles)*
Illustrated with black-and-white photographs and color prints
Silver Burdett, 1967
240 pages, bibliography, index

This book is divided into three sections: Biography, Picture Portfolio, and His Own Words. The biography section provides a summary of Pershing's life in a rather dry, academic tone. It includes Pershing's childhood memories of the Civil War, his early career as a teacher, and his appointment to West Point. He earned a degree in law while serving as a professor of military science at the University of Nebraska and was an instructor at West Point and assistant secretary of war before serving in the Mexican War. He served several terms in the Philippines. Congress granted him the title of General of the Armies in recognition of his service as leader of the American Expeditionary Force during World War I. Highlights of Pershing's life are shown in photographs and reproductions of paintings in the 30-page picture portfolio. The last 110 pages are excerpts from Pershing's memoirs.

John J. Pershing: World War I Hero
Written by John Foster
Illustrated by Herman B. Vestal
Garrard Publishing Company, 1970
112 pages, index

This interesting narrative presents a humanistic view of Pershing. His hardships as a boy, his education at West Point, and his early career in the army on the western frontier and in the Mexican War are well described. He made unprecedented advances in diplomacy through his acceptance of the Philippine people and their customs during a tour of duty there, although he did need to make a show of power as well. He tragically lost his wife and daughters in a fire and was devoted to his surviving son. He kept the American troops together as a unit during World War I in spite of pressure to use U.S. soldiers to bolster dwindling British and French lines. He continued to take an active interest in the military through World War II.

Lawrence of Arabia
Written by Phillip Knightley
Illustrated with black-and-white photographs
Thomas Nelson, Inc., 1977
96 pages, map, index

Welsh-born Thomas Edward Lawrence seemed an unlikely candidate for the legend he became. His lifelong interest in archeology contributed to his recruitment as an agent for the British government in Syria. He adapted well to Arab life, dressing, eating, and living as a native. When the British were looking for leadership in fighting the Turks, Lawrence agreed to help unite the Arabs in the fight, supporting the Arab goal of self-government. He boldly led attacks and missions to disrupt Turkish supply lines by blowing up railroad tracks. His trip to the peace conference proved unsuccessful in obtaining the self-rule he had wanted for the Arabs.

The Many Worlds of Herbert Hoover
Written by James P. Terzian
Julian Messner, 1966
191 pages, index

Hoover's Quaker upbringing influenced his decisions throughout life. Having become wealthy as a mining engineer, he accepted the position of head of the Commission for the Relief of Belgium, refusing to take a salary for this or most other public positions he later held. He was extremely successful in distributing more than five million tons of food, clothing, and medical supplies to devastated countries during the war. He also administered supply distribution to American troops, influencing every phase of food production from soil to stomach. As director of the American Relief Administration in Europe after the war, he oversaw the transport of millions of tons of supplies to war-ravaged areas. Unfortunately, his noteworthy accomplishments have been overshadowed in history because, as president when the depression hit, he was ineffective in solving the huge problems of mass unemployment. Years later, however, President Truman remembered and asked Hoover to assist with worldwide relief programs following World War II.

The True Story of Lawrence of Arabia
Written and illustrated by John Thomas
Children's Press, 1965
141 pages, index of place names

This book focuses on Lawrence's successful destruction of Turkish supply trains. He was an expert at his favorite sport of bridge wrecking. His faithful Arab followers would attack the soldiers aboard a destroyed train and then load their camels with selections from its supplies. Lawrence's successful attack on Akaba and his victory at Damascus are also included. His later years and his disappointment that the peace conference did not grant independence to the Arabs are summarized in the last chapter.

Vladimir Ilich Lenin
(World Leaders: Past & Present Series)
Written by John Haney
Illustrated with black-and-white photographs
Chelsea House Publishers, 1988
112 pages, chronology, bibliography, index

After a brief background of Russian peasants' serfdom and poverty, the account then covers significant aspects of Lenin's childhood that influenced his beliefs. He first studied law, thinking that Russia could be changed through legal means, but decided that revolutionary action was necessary to overthrow the tsarist order. Lenin opposed Russian involvement in World War I, claiming that the workers were dying in a savage and pointless war. When he came into power he signed an armistice with Germany in December 1917 and agreed to the Treaty of Brest-Litovsk in March 1918.

Woodrow Wilson
(World Leaders: Past & Present Series)
Written by J. Perry Leavell, Jr.
Illustrated with black-and-white photographs
Chelsea House Publishers, 1987
116 pages, chronology, bibliography, index

Both the personal and public sides of Wilson's personality and life are presented in an objective manner. The book starts with the declaration of war and then gives background information about Wilson's experiences before becoming president. His early teaching career and presidency of Princeton are discussed. Also included are Wilson's leadership during the war and his attempts at peacemaking, including his bitter disappointment over the defeat of the League of Nations in the Senate. The question of presidential competency is raised because Wilson suffered a stroke, and it is not known how capable he was of making decisions, at least part of the time, during his last year in office.

The Woodrow Wilson Story: An Idealist in Politics
Written by Catherine Owens Peare
Thomas Y. Crowell, 1963
277 pages, bibliography, index

The son of a Presbyterian minister, Woodrow Wilson remained deeply religious throughout his life. As a young boy in Georgia he saw the devastation of the Civil War and the failures of the Reconstruction. He earned a Ph.D. from Johns Hopkins University and taught at Bryn Mawr, Wesleyan University, and Princeton. He was elected governor of New Jersey while serving as president of Princeton, and went on to become president of the United States just as war was brewing. World peace was the great goal of his life, and he had high hopes for his Fourteen Points, especially the League of Nations. But leaders of the victorious nations demanded revenge at the close of the war, and Congress would not approve the entry of the United States into the League of Nations.

Fiction Books

After the Dancing Days
Written by Margaret I. Rostkowski
Harper & Row Publishers, 1986
217 pages

When Annie's father returns from serving in World War I, her mother wants the family to forget the war ever happened and continue on with their lives. That is, of course, impossible. Annie has seen many wounded men being unloaded from the train before her father got off, and her father is a doctor in the hospital where these soldiers are being treated. Annie begins visiting the hospital without her mother's permission and befriends a withdrawn young veteran who has been severely injured and disfigured.

No Hero for the Kaiser
Written by Rudolf Frank
Translated from the German by Patricia Crampton
Illustrated by Klaus Steffens
Lothrop, Lee & Shepard Books, 1986
222 pages

When the Russians and Germans turned the small Polish hamlet of Kopchovka into a battleground, most of the villagers fled. Fourteen-year-old Jan Kubitzky was left to fend for himself in the deserted ruins. German soldiers moved through quickly, taking Jan with them and causing him to serve in the German army for two years. Jan experienced more horror, fear, and misery in that time than he would have thought possible.

Tikhon
Written and illustrated by Ilse-Margaret Vogel
Harper & Row Publishers, 1984
112 pages

Tikhon was one of the many Russian soldiers stranded in Germany after the war. When Inge found him hiding in a basement room in her home, she liked him immediately. They learned words from each other's languages, and Tikhon made a dollhouse replica of Inge's home when he was not busy with chores. Then he was arrested and placed in prison because he had no official papers. Inge was heartbroken for the four months he was gone. One day he appeared and told the family he had escaped. When the police came looking for him, he decided to leave and make his way back home to Russia.

War Horse
Written by Michael Morpurgo
Greenwillow Books, 1982
148 pages

Captain James Nicholls painted a picture of a beautiful horse confiscated for the war effort in 1914. Titled Joey, this picture was the inspiration for a story credibly told from a horse's point of view. Joey begins his war service in Germany, but he is captured and used in France also. His tale graphically describes the hardships of the war for both men and animals. The lack of food and shelter takes its toll on all participants. Joey pulls an ambulance wagon back and forth from the front lines, charges into battle, and survives alone in no-man's-land.

Sample Lesson Plan

Introduction

Read aloud pages 4–7 from *World War I* (Silver Burdett Picture Histories Series) by Pierre Miguel or summarize the information contained on these pages about the background of the war. Then read aloud pages 4–5 from *World War I* (Wars that Changed the World Series) by Ken Hills. Use a world map to discuss the location of the assassination of Archduke Franz Ferdinand and of the Central and Allied Powers. (Page 5 in Hills' book has a clear map for the basis of this discussion.) List questions generated by students about the war on transparencies or chart paper and save for a later session.

Building Background

Meet in the school library. Ask each student to work with a partner to find causes of World War I. Instruction in using the webbing technique, based on placing each major topic on a separate piece of paper and surrounding the topic with related details, may be provided by either the librarian or the classroom teacher. Encourage students to use all the resources of the library to find information. Both the school librarian and the teacher should be actively involved in helping students access, analyze, and record information.

Have students meet in teams of four (two sets of partners). Ask them to construct an outline on chart paper or transparencies listing the major causes of the war and the supporting details. Compare the outlines as a whole group during the latter part of the session.

Issues

How did the wealth and power of European countries affect their interactions with each other? Why were alliances among countries formed? What upset the fragile balance of power that had existed?

Review questions from charts or transparencies generated during the first session. Have all the questions been answered? Students who volunteer to find answers to unanswered questions may receive extra credit.

Major Battles and Turning Points

Begin with a discussion of the events in Europe in the early 1910s. Why was the assassination of Archduke Franz Ferdinand important?

Talk about the Schlieffen Plan. How effective was it once the war began? Discuss the location of and the activity along the Eastern and Western Fronts.

Specific conflicts that could provide topics for research or discussion are the Battles of the Marne, the Battles of Ypres, the Battle of Tannenberg, the Battle of Neuve Chapelle, the Battle for Poland, the Battle of Verdun, the Battle of the Somme, the Battle of Passchendaele, the Battle of Cambrai, the Battle of Caporetto, and the Battle of Lys.

Trench Warfare

Talk about trench warfare. (Pages 22–25 of Miquel's *World War I* have a clear description and diagrams of the trenches.) What were some of the health problems, both physical and emotional, suffered by soldiers in the trenches? Why did trench warfare result in the futile loss of life?

Attack on the Lusitania

Read *Attack on the Lusitania* by Rupert Matthews aloud to the class and discuss the significance of the incident in shaping public opinion about the war in the United States.

Political and Military Leadership

Who were some of the European decision makers? Why did the United States make a late entry into the war? Students may be asked to find additional information on Winston Churchill, Woodrow Wilson, Herbert Hoover, David Lloyd George, Georges Clemenceau, Vladimir Lenin, John J. Pershing, Prince Feisal, and Lawrence of Arabia.

Projects

Distribute a list of recommended research topics and ask students to indicate first, second, and third choices. Collect the papers and make assignments during the next session. Suggested topics include artillery of World War I, trench warfare, the war at sea, the war in the air, methods of communication, espionage, terrorism, development of tanks, caring for the injured, refugees, poisonous gases and gas masks, the Russian Revolution, the Ottoman Empire, reasons for the U.S. entry into the war, and women's roles in the war effort. Additional ideas for projects may be found later in this unit and in the introduction.

Encourage students to plan ways of reporting their information to the rest of the class in an interesting way. Large charts or graphs, transparencies, models, dioramas, and other visual projects enable other students to gain a better understanding of the factual material. Students may begin research in the school library or classroom as appropriate.

Fiction Books

Distribute bibliographies of available fiction books. Tell students they may select one or more books to read for extra credit. They may complete the reporting form for fiction books in Appendix B to capture relevant information and provide a record of books read.

Students who have chosen to read fiction books may share significant aspects of the books with the rest of the class.

Effects of the War

Discuss the Versailles Conference. Who attended? Which countries were not invited to attend? What were the provisions of the treaty? How is the treaty viewed today?

Culminating Activity

The students present the projects they have selected to the class.

Suggested Questions

Why was World War I called the war to end all wars?

Why were the countries of Europe building up their military forces in the early 1900s?

How was the balance of power expected to avoid war?

How did nationalism contribute to the mood for war?

How did military alliances encourage nations to declare war on other nations?

Why was control of the Middle East important to Great Britain?

What were the causes of unrest in Serbia that prompted the assassination of Archduke Franz Ferdinand?

How would the German army's position have been different if the Schlieffen Plan had been followed more accurately?

What were the major causes of the stalemate for much of the war?

What were some of the technological advances in military equipment and machines that came about in an effort to break the stalemate?

How did trench warfare get started?

What were living conditions like for soldiers in the trenches?

How did the military leaders' failure to recognize new weapons contribute to the casualties of the war?

Why did some of the French soldiers mutiny and how was the mutiny resolved?

Why did the Russian people and the new Soviet government want to withdraw from the war?

In what ways did the home front become as dangerous as the battlefront for many people during the war?

Where was Adolf Hitler during World War I?

Why did the United States wait until 1917 to officially enter the war?

What were the reasons for the United States entry into the war?

In what ways was General Pershing well qualified to command the American Expeditionary Forces in the war?

How did the contributions of women in the work force during the war change attitudes about women's place in society after the war?

Why did Prince Feisal feel the peace conference was unfair to Arabs?

What were President Wilson's Fourteen Points?

How might world history have been different if the leaders at the peace conference had accepted Wilson's proposals?

In what ways was Wilson an idealist?

How did Wilson's refusal to compromise contribute to the Senate's failure to approve the League of Nations he desperately wanted?

How did the Treaty of Versailles sow the seeds of World War II?

Suggested Activities

Make a chart contrasting the strengths and weaknesses of the Allies and the Central Powers at the beginning of the war.

Write a report on one of the major countries involved in the war. Cover the period just prior to 1914 and continue to 1919.

Make a model of a trench system along the western front.

Make a gas mask and write an explanation of why gas masks were needed during the war.

Make a model of a submarine.

Make a diorama of the Battle of Jutland.

Create a picture book of the air aces in World War I.

Write a diary that could have been kept by the Red Baron.

Make a chart showing the roles women played in the war.

Write a diary that could have been kept by a refugee who was forced from his or her home.

Dramatize a meeting between the Big Four at the Paris Peace Conference.

Design a chart showing the economic impact of the war on the nations involved.

Dramatize a debate that could have been held in the U.S. Senate concerning U.S. involvement in the League of Nations.

Make a chart comparing the League of Nations and the United Nations.

Glossary

ace—A pilot who shot down five or more enemy planes.

Allied Powers—France, Great Britain, Russia, and other countries that fought against Germany and Austria-Hungary in the war.

allies—Countries that are united with each other during war.

American Expeditionary Force—The United States 1st Division and Marine Brigade, sent to Europe under the command of General John J. Pershing.

armistice—An official, but temporary, end to fighting in a war; a truce.

artillery—Large guns and cannons on wheels, often operated from the trenches.

balance of power—A deterrent to war based upon opposing alliances being roughly equal in strength.

barbed wire—Twisted wire armed with barbs or sharp points.

battalion—A unit of about 1,000 men led by a lieutenant-colonel.

bayonet—Knife-like weapon that could be clipped to the muzzle of a rifle for close combat.

Big Bertha—Large German gun that shot shells up to 75 miles.

Big Four—U.S. President Woodrow Wilson, British Prime Minister David Lloyd George, French Premier Georges Clemenceau, and Italian Prime Minister Vittorio Orlando.

billets—Living quarters for soldiers in civilian homes.

Bolsheviks—Followers of Lenin's version of Marxism who seized the Russian government in November 1917.

bombard—Drop bombs or attack heavily with artillery fire.

booby trap—A hidden mine or grenade set to go off if disturbed.

brigade—Four battalions commanded by a brigadier general.

casualties—The number of men killed, captured, wounded, or missing in battles.

cavalry—An army unit mounted on horseback or moving in motor vehicles and assigned to combat missions that require great mobility.

censorship—The deletion from communications (letters and newspapers) of information that army officials consider to be harmful as general knowledge or useful to the enemy.

Central Powers—Austria-Hungary and Germany.

company—A unit of 250 soldiers led by a captain.

convoy system—Cargo ships escorted by warships.

deadlock—A period of time in which neither side gains much ground in the war.

deserter—A member of the military who leaves his duty station without permission.

division—Three infantry brigades plus supporting units (18,700 men) commanded by a major-general.

dogfight—Air battle between enemy aircraft.

draft—To conscript for military service.

Dreadnought—The first modern battleship; launched by the British in 1906. Similar ships were called dreadnoughts.

duckboards—Wooden planking, similar to flat ladders, laid on the bottom of trenches.

dugout—An underground room dug below trench walls.

eastern front—The line of fighting in between Germany and Russia in eastern Europe.

espionage—Spying to collect military secrets.

flamethrower—A weapon made of a portable tank of oil with a hose that squirted a spray of flame many yards long.

Fokker plane—The first plane in which a machine gun was synchronized with the propeller; invented for the Germans by a Dutch scientist.

Fourteen Points—A set of war aims proposed by U.S. President Woodrow Wilson designed to bring about a just peace settlement and set forth principles for preventing future wars.

fraternization—Associating with enemy soldiers.

gas mask—Protective face covering for soldiers exposed to dangerous fumes from chlorine and other gases released by the enemy during battles.

hand grenade—A small, powerful, hand-thrown bomb.

howitzer—A big gun that fired heavy shells in a high arc.

immigrants—People who leave one country to settle and live in another country.

infantry—Soldiers who are trained and equipped to fight on foot.

inflation—A rise in prices beyond the value of available goods.

isolationism—A national policy of abstention from alliances and other political and economic relations with other countries.

kaiser—German emperor.

land mines—Buried explosives set to go off if disturbed.

League of Nations—An association of nations organized to solve problems between countries without warfare.

liberty bonds—U.S. war bonds sold during World War I.

Lusitania—A British passenger ship that was sunk by a German U-boat when sailing from New York to Liverpool in 1915.

machine gun—An automatic gun that uses small-arms ammunition for rapid, continuous firing.

maim—Serious physical injury which results in the loss of a body part or disfiguration of the body; the act of inflicting serious physical injury.

military alliance—An agreement with one or more countries that, in case of attack, other members of the alliance will come to the attacked country's aid.

mobilize—Call troops together and prepare for battle.

mutiny—Soldiers refusing to obey orders of officers.

nationalism—An exaggerated form of patriotism based on the belief in the superiority of one's own country and government.

navy—A nation's ships of war and logistic support.

neutral—Neither on one side nor on the other; nations that do not take sides in a war.

no-man's-land—The contested strip of ground separating the most advanced trenches of opposing armies.

offensive—An attack.

pacifist—A person who is against war and believes that peaceful methods should be used to settle conflicts.

periscope—A tube with a lens through which a submarine crew member can see above the water without surfacing the craft.

platoon—A unit of about 60 men led by a junior officer.

propaganda—Information spread by a government to improve its position or to undermine the enemy's position.

rear—The area farthest from the fighting.

Red Baron—Germany's war ace, Baron Manfred von Richthofen, who shot down 80 airplanes.

refugees—People who have fled their own countries during war.

sabotage—Damage done behind the enemy's lines to slow down the enemy's war effort.

sapper—A soldier who works at building trenches and other fortifications.

shell shock—An acute stress syndrome resulting from active combat, caused by fear and the constant noise of fighting.

sniper—An expert marksman who killed soldiers if their heads appeared above the parapet.

stalemate—A position in which movement is impossible and neither side can win.

Supreme War Council—A strategy planning group for the Allies.

tank—A heavy armored vehicle fitted with guns; developed by the British to cross wire entanglements and trenches under fire.

Tommies—Nickname for British soldiers; based on a fictitious name for a soldier used in a sample army account book in 1829.

torpedoes—Underwater missiles fired by submarines or ships.

Treaty of Brest-Litovsk—An agreement that forced the Soviet Union to give up large amounts of territory to Germany in return for Soviet withdrawal from the war.

trench—A long cut in the ground with the excavated dirt thrown up front; used for military defense.

trench warfare—Warfare in which the opposing forces attack and counterattack from a relatively permanent system of trenches protected by barbed wire entanglements.

Triple Alliance—An agreement among the countries of Germany, Austria-Hungary, and Italy that each would come to the other's aid if attacked by another country.

Triple Entente—A friendly agreement between Great Britain, France, and Russia that opened the discussion of joint military plans, although it carried no pledges of military support.

ultimatum—Final proposition or demands of either party in a dispute.

victory gardens—Vegetable gardens planted by U.S. citizens to alleviate the problem of food shortages caused by the war.

war bonds—Money borrowed from citizens to support the war effort.

western front—The main war zone in northern France and Belgium; a line of trenches running 475 miles from the North Sea to the Swiss border.

Yankees—Nickname for soldiers from the United States.

Zimmerman note—Intercepted by the British, this message written by Germany's foreign minister to the German ambassador in Mexico encouraged Mexico to begin fighting with the United States.

World War II Literature Unit

Selected Chronology

1919	The Treaty of Versailles ended World War I.
1920	The League of Nations was formed in Geneva, Switzerland; the United States, the Soviet Union, and Germany were not members.
1925	The Allies agreed to sponsor Germany for membership in the League of Nations and to begin disarmament.
1928	National leaders met in Paris and signed the Kellogg-Briand Pact outlawing war.
1929	The depression began in the United States. Joseph Stalin became dictator of the Soviet Union.
1931	The Japanese army invaded and occupied Manchuria, China.
1932	Franklin Delano Roosevelt elected president of the United States.
1933	Adolf Hitler became chancellor of Germany. Japan attacked the Chinese cities of Peking and Tientsin.
1935	Italian troops invaded Ethiopia. Germany and Japan left the League of Nations.
1936	Germany and Italy formed an alliance. Hitler sent troops into demilitarized Rhineland. Beginning of the Spanish Civil War, which lasted until 1939.
1937	Italy left the League of Nations.
1938	German soldiers united Austria with Germany. Munich Agreement gave the Sudetenland of Czechoslovakia to Germany.
1939	Hitler seized the rest of Czechoslovakia.

	August 23	Germany and the Soviet Union signed a nonagression pact.
	September 1	Germany invaded Poland.
	September 3	Great Britain and France declared war on Germany.
	September 10	Canada declared war on Germany.
	November 30	The Soviet Union invaded Finland.
1940	April–June	Germany conquered Denmark and Norway.
	May 10	Winston Churchill became prime minister of England.
	May	Belgium, Luxembourg, and the Netherlands fell to Germany.
	May 27–June 4	Allied soldiers evacuated from Dunkirk.
	June 10	Italy declared war on France and Great Britain.
	June 22	France signed an armistice with Germany.
	July 10	Battle of Britain began.
	September 7	Beginning of German blitz on British cities.
	September	Italy invaded Egypt.
	October	Italy invaded Greece.
	December	Beginning of British offensive in North Africa.
1941	February	Rommel and the Afrika Korps arrived in Tripoli.
	March	U.S. Congress approved the Lend-Lease Act.
	April 6	Germany invaded Greece and Yugoslavia.
	May	Germany invaded Crete.
	June 22	Germany invaded the Soviet Union.
	August	Roosevelt and Churchill issued the Atlantic Charter.
	September 8	German troops completed the blockade of Leningrad, which continued through January 1944.
	December 7	The Japanese attacked the U.S. Pacific Fleet in Pearl Harbor.
	December 8	The United States, Canada, and Great Britain declared war on Japan.
	December 9	China declared war on the Axis nations.
	December 11	Germany and Italy declared war on the United States.
1942	January	The U.S. Attorney General issued proclamations prohibiting enemy aliens from living in over 100 zones in the western U.S. in which sabotage was feared.
	February 15	Singapore fell to the Japanese.
	February 19	President Roosevelt signed Executive Order No. 9066 giving the military the right to evacuate Japanese-Americans from the western U.S.
	March 18	The War Relocation Authority was established to supervise the orderly evacuation of the Japanese from the west coast.

	June	120,000 Japanese-Americans were evacuated from their homes to relocation camps.
	June 4–6	The Allies defeated Japan in the Battle of Midway.
	August 7	U.S. marines landed on Guadalcanal.
	August 25	Hitler ordered his forces to capture Stalingrad.
	October 23	British forces attacked the Axis at El Alamein in Egypt.
	November 8	Allied troops landed in Algeria and Morocco.
1943	January	Roosevelt and Churchill announced that the Allies would accept only unconditional surrender from the Axis powers.
	February 2	The last German troops in Stalingrad surrendered.
	May	Axis forces in northern Africa surrendered.
	July	The Allies invaded Sicily.
	September 3	Italy secretly surrendered to the Allies.
	September 9	Allied troops landed at Salerno, Italy.
	November	Roosevelt, Churchill, and Stalin met to discuss the invasion of France.
1944	June 6	D-Day; Allied troops invaded Normandy in France.
	July 20	A plot to assassinate Hitler failed.
	December	The Battle of the Bulge.
1945	April	Franklin Roosevelt died; Harry Truman became president of the United States.
	April 30	Hitler committed suicide in Berlin.
	May 7	Germany surrendered to the Allies in Rheims, France, ending World War II in Europe.
	June	U.S. Marines defeated the Japanese at Okinawa.
	August 6	The U.S. dropped the atomic bomb on Hiroshima.
	August 8	The Soviet Union declared war on Japan and invaded Manchuria.
	August 9	The U.S. dropped a bomb on Nagasaki.
	August 14	Japan surrendered.
	September 2	V-J Day; Japan signed the official statement of surrender.

Recommended Books

Picture Books

The Angel with a Mouth-Organ
Written by Christobel Mattingley
Illustrated by Astra Lacis
Hodder & Stoughton, Limited (Australia), 1984
Holiday House, Inc. (U.S.), 1986
30 pages

As a mother and her two children are decorating their Christmas tree, the children ask her to tell them the angel story. She recalls her family's flight from their home after a bombing raid destroys their village. The setting is not specified, but appears to be somewhere in Europe. They walk for many days, using all their food and finding no place to stay. One day the soldiers take her father away even though he has only one arm. The mother and her two daughters are taken to a refugee camp in boxcars and stay there until they are reunited with their father, who is carrying the glass angel with him.

The Children We Remember
Written by Chana Byers Abells
Illustrated with photographs from the archives of Yad Vashem, The Holo-
    caust Martyrs' and Heroes' Remembrance Authority, Jerusalem, Israel
Greenwillow Books, 1983
48 pages

Compelling black-and-white photographs portray the tragedy of Jewish children during World War II. Accompanied by a brief, controlled text.

Faithful Elephants: A True Story of Animals, People, and War
Written by Yukio Tsuchiya
Translated from the Japanese by Tomoko Tsuchiya
Illustrated by Ted Levin
Houghton Mifflin Company, 1988
32 pages

A deeply moving story about the elephants who starved to death rather than eat the poisoned food that was given to potentially dangerous animals when fire raids were destroying Tokyo.

The army feared that wild animals would be released from their cages and be a danger to people if the zoo were hit.

Hiroshima No Pika
Written by Toshi Maruki
Translated from the Japanese through Komine Shoten Co., Ltd.
Illustrated by Toshi Maruki
Lothrop, Lee & Shepard Books, 1980
48 pages

Through the experiences of a young girl of the time, this book vividly illustrates the horror, the tragedy, and the long-term effects of the atomic bomb dropped on Hiroshima in 1945.

The Journey
Written and illustrated by Sheila Hamanaka
Orchard Books, 1990
40 pages, index

The story of a five-panel mural (8' x 25') depicting the history of Japanese-Americans, as well as the artist's personal inquiry into events in her family's life, are portrayed in folktale fashion. Reproductions from the painting are accompanied by a concise text describing the hardships of early Japanese immigrants, the imprisonment of Japanese-Americans during World War II, and the continuing struggle for the equity of Japanese people in the United States.

My Daddy Was a Soldier: A World War II Story
Written and illustrated by Deborah Kogan Ray
Holiday House, 1990
40 pages

A summary of the effects of the war on the United States as expressed through a young girl whose father is drafted into the army. Mentions food and gasoline rationing, victory gardens, working mothers, and other aspects of wartime.

My Hiroshima

Written and illustrated by Junko Morimoto
Viking, 1987
32 pages

Morimoto recalls her early childhood in the beautiful city of Hiroshima. The war started when she was in fourth grade, and there were changes in her life due to shortages of materials and the need for military exercises. She was in high school in 1945 and vividly recalls the dropping of the atomic bomb. She describes the terror and the horror in both words and pictures. The book ends with a plea that this evil not be repeated.

The Number on My Grandfather's Arm

Written by David Adler
Illustrated with family photographs by Rose Eichenbaum
UAHC Press, 1987
28 pages

A young girl learns about concentration camp experiences in a very personal way as her grandfather answers her questions about the number on his arm. Black-and-white photographs of Sigfried Halbreich and Rose Eichenbaum's granddaughter accompany the factual text.

Rose Blanche

Written by Roberto Innocenti and Christope Gallaz
Translated from the Italian by Martha Coventry and Richard Graglia
Illustrated by Roberto Innocenti
Creative Education, Inc., 1985
32 pages

This story, set in Germany, provides a child's sense of being aware of the war without understanding what is happening. Starkly realistic illustrations show her discovery of a concentration camp and her secret sharing of her food—until the arrival of the Allied troops.

Factual Books

Air Raid—Pearl Harbor! The Story of December 7, 1941
Written by Theodore Taylor
Illustrated by W. T. Mars
Thomas Y. Crowell, 1971
186 pages, bibliography, index
Presents the dramatic story of the attack that destroyed the majority of the U.S. Pacific Fleet, told from the viewpoint of both Japan and the United States. A list of key figures in the story of Pearl Harbor is included.

America in World War II: 1941
Written by Edward F. Dolan
Illustrated with black-and-white and color photographs
The Millbrook Press, 1991
72 pages, maps, bibliography, index
A detailed account of the attack on Pearl Harbor describes the background, the bombings, and the reactions. The subsequent attack on the Philippines and the entry of the United States into World War II are also explained well. Photographs of decision makers of the time with brief biographical notes are featured throughout the book.

Behind Barbed Wire: The Imprisonment of Japanese-Americans during World War II
Written by Daniel S. Davis
Illustrated with black-and-white photographs
E. P. Dutton, 1982
166 pages, bibliography, index
The history of discrimination against the Japanese people in the United States is summarized. After Pearl Harbor some War Department officials and congressmen proposed the removal of the Japanese from the West Coast. Most Californians agreed, fearing their state would be the next target for attack. President Roosevelt signed an executive order authorizing the War Relocation Authority, and Japanese-Americans were forced to leave valuable possessions behind and evacuate their homes. U.S. citizenship was ignored, and all Japanese were treated like prisoners of war. The people tried to make homes out of barren barracks and communities out

of chaos. When the war was over many had no place to go and no means of support.

Bismarck!
(A First Book Series)
Written by Frank Sloan
Illustrated with black-and-white and color photographs
Franklin Watts, 1991
64 pages, maps, glossary, bibliography, index

The history of the *Bismarck* is clearly described, following a brief review of the war to that point. The *Bismarck* was launched by the Germans on 18 May 1941 and traveled to the Atlantic Ocean where it engaged in a number of sea battles with British warships before it was sunk on 27 May. The last chapter describes the discovery of the *Bismarck* on the ocean floor off the coast of France in 1989.

Blitzkrieg!
(Witness History Series)
Written by Peter Chrisp
Illustrated with black-and-white and color photographs
The Bookwright Press, 1991
63 pages, maps, chronology, glossary, bibliography, index

A description of the elements of blitzkrieg is followed by a concise summary of the major events of the war, highlighting blitzkrieg in various countries. Photographs and brief biographies of seven leading figures are included.

Blitzkrieg
(World War II 50th Anniversary Series)
Written by Wallace B. Black and Jean F. Blashfield
Illustrated with black-and-white photographs
Crestwood House, 1991
48 pages, maps, glossary, index

Following a brief history of the beginning of the war, blitzkrieg warfare is described with several examples. The so-called phony war, the war in Scandinavia, the war in France, and the miracle at Dunkirk are each discussed. Three sections of photographs feature famous leaders, German panzer vehicles, and German aircraft.

D-Day: Turning Points in American History
Written by Marilyn Miller
Illustrated with black-and-white and color photographs
Silver Burdett, 1986
64 pages, maps, bibliography, index

After a brief summary of Eisenhower's leadership and decisions concerning the project, the events of the Allied invasion of German-occupied France from the beaches of Normandy are described in some detail. Clearly marked maps aid in the explanation of the complicated maneuvers.

The Holocaust: The Fire That Raged
Written by Seymour Rossel
Illustrated with black-and-white photographs
Franklin Watts, 1989
124 pages, maps, chronology, bibliography, index

A clear description of what happened to European Jews during the war. Questions concerning how this could have been allowed to happen and whether it could happen again are discussed. A chart of death toll statistics is included.

Never To Forget: The Jews of the Holocaust
Written by Milton Meltzer
Harper & Row Publishers, 1976
217 pages, chronology, bibliography, index, death toll statistics

A careful report of the history of hatred in Germany, the planned destruction of the Jewish people, and the spirit of resistance expressed in a way that personalizes the disaster by discussing people as well as statistics.

A Nightmare in History: The Holocaust 1933–1945
Written by Miriam Chaikin
Illustrated with black-and-white photographs and prints
Clarion Books, 1987
150 pages, bibliography, index

Documents the courage and strength of Jews during the Nazi era. Discusses the history of prejudice against the Jewish people, and describes the ghettos and death camps.

Overlord: D-Day and the Invasion of Europe
Written by Albert Marrin
Illustrated with black-and-white photographs
Atheneum, 1982
177 pages, maps, bibliography, index

Relates the planning of the invasion of Nazi-occupied France across the English Channel. Major landings and battles are described, including the advances and retreats of both armies and the eventual victory of the Allies over the Germans.

Pearl Harbor
(Great Mysteries: Opposing Viewpoints Series)
Written by Deborah Bachrach
Illustrated with black-and-white photographs
Greenhaven Press, Inc., 1989
112 pages, maps, bibliography, index

After a brief description of the attack on Pearl Harbor, some of the problems between Japan and the United States are described. The narrative then turns to such issues as whether or not the attack was really a surprise, how much responsibility the U.S. generals and Navy officers may have had for the tragedy, and the possible consequences of withheld secret information. Conflicting viewpoints on all of these subjects are presented. No answers are given; it is a thought-provoking presentation.

Pearl Harbor: Turning Points of World War II
Written by William E. Shapiro
Illustrated with black-and-white photographs
Franklin Watts, 1984
103 pages, maps, chronology, bibliography, index

A description of the attack on Pearl Harbor is followed by some background information concerning the deterioration of the U.S. relationship with Japan and the U.S. isolationist policy concerning the war to that point. A more detailed explanation of the attack's consequences and a look at the event in retrospect are included.

Prisoners of War
(World at War Series)
Written by Conrad Stein
Illustrated with black-and-white photographs
Children's Press, 1987
48 pages, index

An estimated 15 million men and women were captured and held prisoner during World War II. Their fate in prison camps was a grim lottery. Those captured by U.S. forces were fed and treated well. The worst defiance of the Geneva Convention took place in German and Russian prison camps. Many Americans suffered ill treatment and starvation at the hands of the Japanese. The Bataan Death March in the Philippines is given as one example. Conditions within POW camps throughout the world are described.

Rescue: The Story of How Gentiles Saved Jews in the Holocaust
Written by Milton Meltzer
Harper & Row Publishers, 1988
168 pages, maps, bibliography, index

A summary of the historic prejudice against Jews is followed by descriptions of 12 heroic acts performed by Gentile men and women in saving Jewish people from Hitler's final solution. The rescuers featured were from Germany, Poland, the Soviet Union, France, Italy, the Netherlands, and Denmark, the nation of rescuers.

Second World War
(Conflict in the 20th Century Series)
Written by Charles Messenger
Edited by Dr. John Pimlott
Illustrated with black-and-white and color photographs
Franklin Watts, 1987
62 pages, bibliography, index

This book provides a concise summary of major military maneuvers and battles and clearly describes the escalation of conflict into a major world war.

The Second World War
(Events of Yesteryear Series)
Written by Michel Pierre and Annette Wieviorka
Translated from the French by Christopher Sharp
Illustrated with black-and-white and color photographs
Silver Burdett, 1987
70 pages, maps, chronology, glossary, index

Includes brief accounts of a wide variety of topics. The major battles, events, and fronts are each presented in a two-page spread of descriptive text. Appropriate photographs and illustrations complement the narrative.

Sinister Touches: The Secret War against Hitler
Written by Robert Goldstein
Dial Press, 1982
214 pages, bibliography, index

This fascinating account of the secret war against the Nazis has the mystery and intrigue of a spy novel. The cracking of the Nazi codes, espionage and daring missions throughout the world, and the race for the atomic bomb present an engrossing view of the war that could not be told until after it was over.

Smoke and Ashes: The Story of the Holocaust
Written by Barbara Rogasky
Illustrated with black-and-white photographs
Holiday House, 1988
187 pages, maps, glossary, bibliography, index

Presents a brief overview of the roots of anti-Semitism and Hitler's rise to power. Ghettos, concentration and death camps, and the reality of life for Jews during this period are vividly described. Examples of Jewish resistance are included. The question of why the United States or Great Britain did not intercede is explored.

The Third Reich
(Witness History Series)
Written by David Williamson
Illustrated with black-and-white photographs and color prints
The Bookwright Press, 1989
63 pages, maps, glossary, bibliography, index

The Third Reich is analyzed from its beginnings at the close of World War I through its collapse at the end of World War II. The rise of the Nazi party, Hitler's ascent to power, his foreign policies, and the impact of World War II on Germany are discussed. Charts of important dates and brief biographical sketches of leading figures are included.

We Remember the Holocaust
Written by David Adler
Illustrated with black-and-white photographs
Henry Holt and Company, Inc., 1989
148 pages, maps, chronology, bibliography, index

Conceived as an introduction to the history of the Holocaust, Adler expanded his scope to include many of the personal tragedies of the Jewish people. The text is based on interviews with survivors and their relatives. Many of the people he talked with agreed to have precious family photographs reproduced for inclusion in the book. These are supplemented with photographs from the national archives.

World at War: The Holocaust
Written by Conrad Stein
Consultant: Robert L. Messer, Ph.D.
Illustrated with black-and-white photographs
Children's Press, 1986
48 pages, chronology, index

A significant collection of photographs relates the atrocities of the war. The text is brief and supportive of the pictured information.

Biographies

Alicia: My Story
Written by Alicia Appleman-Jerman
Bantam Books, Doubleday Publishing Company, 1988
433 pages

Alicia's story begins in 1938 in the Polish city of Buczacz, when she was eight years old, and continues through 1949 to Israel. Alicia reveals the horrors of the war and her personal courage in surviving it. The reader suffers her loss as her father and four brothers are killed. Although she helps her mother survive in the fields for several months, Alicia eventually witnesses her murder as well. Surviving the war was only part of the battle. She then courageously helped many Jewish people escape to Israel and served two years in the Israeli navy during that country's war of independence.

Anne Frank: Life in Hiding
Written by Johanna Hurwitz
Illustrated by Vera Rosenberry
The Jewish Publication Society, 1988
62 pages, chronology, index

This book presents a summary of Anne Frank's life, including background information from before the beginning of her diary and going beyond the diary to her internment in Auschwitz and her death in Bergen-Belsen.

Anne Frank: The Diary of a Young Girl
Written by Anne Frank
Translated from the Dutch by B. M. Mooyaart-Doubleday
Introduction by Eleanor Roosevelt
Doubleday Publishing Company, 1967
308 pages

The Frank family thought they had escaped Hitler's cruelty when they relocated from Germany to Holland, but they were soon forced into hiding. Anne recorded the daily living routines and her personal thoughts as they remained in their hidden apartment for 25 months.

As the Waltz Was Ending
Written by Emma Macalik Butterworth
Four Winds Press, 1982
187 pages

This autobiography of an Austrian girl describes Vienna prior to the war, the girl's joy in being selected for the ballet school of the Vienna State Opera at the age of eight, and the beginning of her promising career as a ballerina. All of this changed abruptly when the German army invaded Austria. She relates the fear of bombing raids, the destruction of the beautiful city she loved, and the tragic loss of friends and family members. In 1945 she married a paratrooper from the United States.

The Buck Stops Here: A Biography of Harry Truman
Written by Morrie Greenberg
Illustrated with black-and-white photographs
Dillon Press, Inc., 1989
127 pages, bibliography, index

When Harry Truman became president, he was faced with one of the most significant decisions in the history of the United States—whether or not to use atomic bombs to hasten the end of the war with Japan. This biography presents Truman as a decisive man dedicated to doing what he thought was right. He made that decision and many others without looking back. Having fought in World War I, he found himself making momentous decisions in World War II and also dealing with the conflict in Korea.

The Cage
Written by Ruth Minsky Sender
Macmillan Publishing Company, 1986
245 pages

This well-written autobiography vividly describes the horror and frustration of being removed from a comfortable home to a ghetto, struggling to keep family together, and facing starvation daily. Sender lost touch with her mother and brothers on the day they were transported to the concentration camps and never heard from them again. Although she suffered hunger and illness in the camp, she was spared from death because of her writing ability. She wrote poems expressing feelings of both despair and hope—poems that were valued by supervisors as well as her fellow prisoners.

Churchill and the British
Written by John Bradley
Illustrated with black-and-white photographs
Gloucester Press, 1990
62 pages, maps, chronology, glossary, bibliography, index

Born in 1874, Winston Churchill was the first son of a beautiful American woman and an English lord. After successfully attending prep school, he trained for the army and become an officer. His talent for writing and speaking soon surfaced, and he became a popular war correspondent during the Boer War. His political career began when he was elected to Parliament at the age of 26. He served in various political offices until he became prime minister in 1940. He played a major role in making decisions during World War II, and England recognized his many contributions with knighthood in 1953.

Dwight D. Eisenhower
(World Leaders: Past & Present Series)
Written by Peter Lars Sandberg
Illustrated with black-and-white photographs
Chelsea House Publishers, 1986
116 pages, chronology, bibliography, index

This story of Eisenhower's life begins with the invasion of France and his role as supreme commander of the Allied Expeditionary Force in Europe. His childhood and education at West Point are covered briefly. The peacetime army was greatly reduced after World War I, but Eisenhower was fortunate to serve under brilliant generals during that time, including General Pershing. He was surprised to be selected to command the American forces in the Philippines after Pearl Harbor. His victory as commander of Operation Overlord is described in some detail. His campaign for the presidency and his terms in office conclude the book.

Dwight D. Eisenhower: A Man Called Ike
Written by Jean Darby
Illustrated with black-and-white photographs
Lerner Publications Company, 1989
112 pages, maps, glossary, bibliography, index

Eisenhower's childhood in Kansas and his time at West Point are summarized. He was disappointed to miss seeing action in World War I. His duty posts took him to Panama, Paris, Washington state, the Philippines, and Washington, D.C., between the wars. After Pearl Harbor he was placed in charge of the Far Eastern Section of the War Plans Division. He was then assigned to North Africa, before becoming the commander of Operation Overlord in England. While supervising U.S. occupation in Germany, he pleaded with President Truman not to drop bombs on Japan. After the war he was commander of NATO until friends persuaded him to run for president. He served two terms from 1952 to 1960.

Elie Wiesel: Messenger from the Holocaust
Written by Carol Greene
Illustrated with black-and-white photographs
Children's Press, 1987
32 pages

A brief biography of Elie Wiesel, the winner of the 1986 Nobel Peace Prize, who was the first person to use the term *holocaust* for the destruction of Jewish people. He has dedicated his life to telling and writing about this event, so people will not forget. Includes the text of Wiesel's acceptance speech for the Nobel Peace Prize and a timeline of his life.

The Endless Steppe: Growing Up in Siberia
Written by Esther Hautzig
Thomas Y. Crowell, 1968
243 pages

Hautzig's joyful childhood in Poland came to an unexpected end when her family was arrested and sent to Siberia. She describes the uncomfortable journey in a filthy cattle car in stifling heat. Living conditions were harsh and food was difficult to find, but the story has an upbeat tone. Hautzig found beauty to enjoy in that barren place and came to treasure friends and family.

Franklin Delano Roosevelt

Written by Russell Freedman
Illustrated with black-and-white photographs
Clarion Books, 1990
200 pages, bibliography, index

Roosevelt's tremendous contribution to the history of our country is revealed in this well-written biography. His childhood, early political career, and first terms as president are presented in the first half of the book. The remaining chapters focus on his involvement in the far-reaching decisions necessary to the war effort on the part of the United States. His genuine optimism and initiative in taking action are evident throughout.

Heroes of World War II

(Tales of Courage Series)
Written by Neil Grant
Illustrated by Francis Phillipps
Steck-Vaughn Company, 1989
48 pages, index

Unsung heroes from throughout the world are featured in this book. Included are such diverse people as Witold Pilecki of the Polish underground; Captain Edward Fogarty Fegen, commander of the *Jervis Bay*; Richard Sorge, a German spy for the Soviet Union in Japan; and Ernie Pyle, a U.S. newspaper reporter in England. Fifty such heroes are cited in a biographical listing at the back of the book.

Hitler and the Third Reich

Written by Catherine Bradley
Illustrated with black-and-white photographs
Gloucester Press, 1990
62 pages, maps, chronology, glossary, bibliography, index

A very brief summary of Hitler's life and some of the major battles of the war. His obsession with destroying the Jewish people and his unstable personality are mentioned.

I Am a Star: Child of the Holocaust
Written by Inge Auerbacher
Illustrated with black-and-white photographs
Prentice-Hall, Simon & Schuster, Inc., 1986
87 pages, chronology, bibliography

Written in a conversational tone, this book is intended to serve as a children's introduction to the Holocaust. Auerbacher refers to her happy childhood in southern Germany before the age of eight. Then she and her family were taken to the Terezin concentration camp in Czechoslovakia. She was one of the few survivors. Interspersed with her history of the persecution of the German people and Hitler's rise to power are poems written in the concentration camp. Photographs are from Kulturamt-Stadtarchiv, Landeshauptstadt Stuttgart, State Jewish Museum in Prague, and the YIVO Institute for Jewish Research.

In Kindling Flame: The Story of Hannah Senesh, 1921–1944
Written by Linda Atkinson
Illustrated with black-and-white photographs
Lothrop, Lee & Shepard Books, 1985
214 pages, bibliography, index

Based mainly on diaries and letters written by Senesh, this account of a young Hungarian Jewish woman reveals her exuberance for life even as she chose to become part of the resistance movement that led inevitably to her death at the age of 23.

Joseph Stalin and Communist Russia
Written by Wyatt Blassingame
Illustrated with black-and-white photographs
Garrard Publishing Company, 1971
175 pages, chronology, glossary, index

Stalin's life story is intertwined with the history of Russia. As an abused child, he learned to hate early in life and became involved in the revolutionary movement at a young age. He built a personal political empire during the Russian Revolution and seized power when Lenin died. His role as a world leader during the war, including his objectives for himself and his country, are described.

Mischling, Second Degree: My Childhood in Nazi Germany
Written by Ilse Koehn
Greenwillow Books, 1977
240 pages

Born in Berlin in 1929, Ilse Koehn was four years old when Hitler came to power. As her story progresses she becomes vaguely aware of the first big secret in her life, that her parents are Social Democrats opposed to Hitler. But she does not learn the second secret until after the war, that her father's grandparents were Jewish. Ilse is treated like any other German schoolgirl throughout the war. She vividly describes the three different evacuation camps she is sent to: two in Czechoslovakia and one on the island of Ruegen. Sponsored by the Nazi party, these camps were designed to indoctrinate the young in propaganda of the Hitler regime. Ilse became an unwilling member of the Hitler Youth Organization. Although she was recognized for her leadership abilities, she avoided actually becoming a leader in the movement. Her account of the end of the war, with the constant air raids and bombings, is terrifying. Her German grandmother astutely hides Ilse and her mother for over a month when the Russians invade Berlin, thus saving them from the terrors that befell most German girls and women.

Nazi Hunter: Simon Wiesenthal
Written by Iris Noble
Julian Messner, 1979
158 pages, bibliography, index

Barely escaping death on several occasions, Wiesenthal survived the atrocities of the Holocaust and devoted his life to locating SS leaders and bringing them to justice.

**The Other Victims: First-Person Stories
of Non-Jews Persecuted by the Nazis**
Written by Ina R. Friedman
Houghton Mifflin Company, 1990
214 pages, bibliography, index

Citing the fact that five million non-Jews were killed by the Nazis in addition to the six million Jews exterminated, Friedman proceeds to tell the stories of 11 of these survivors. She has included people persecuted because they were Gypsies, blacks, homosexuals, dissenters, or of strong religious faith. Others refused steriliza-tion and forced labor. As a warning to forgetful generations after the war, both the introduction and the postscript explore Hitler's goal of creating a master race by eliminating all types of people he considered defective.

The Rise and Fall of Adolf Hitler
Written by William Shirer
Random House and Scholastic, 1961
188 pages, index

Written in a conversational tone by Shirer, who was in Berlin throughout the war and was acquainted with Hitler, this biography accurately reveals the full scope of the dictator's life. His unhealthy relationships with people are described, beginning with his father and continuing until his death. Hitler's aversion to holding a steady job and his obsessive need to find scapegoats for his problems help explain some of the possible motivations behind his odious actions. The major events of the war are recounted as they would have appeared from Hitler's viewpoint. Major details of the events leading up to and including his death provide a fitting conclusion to the book.

The Short Life of Sophie Scholl
Written by Hermann Vinke
Illustrated with black-and-white photographs and illustrations
Harper & Row Publishers, 1984
192 pages

Chronicles the brief existence of the White Rose, a nonviolent student group dedicated to spreading the truth about the Nazi regime. Sophie and her brother were both executed by the Nazis for their participation in the movement.

To Life
Written by Ruth Minsky Sender
Macmillan Publishing Company, 1988
228 pages

In this sequel to *The Cage*, Sender poignantly describes the aftermath of the war. Having survived the death camp, she had no place to go and ended up in a concentration camp in Germany. She married a fellow survivor, and they remained in refugee camps until they successfully located a relative who sponsored their trip to the United States.

Vive de Gaulle: The Story of Charles de Gaulle
Written by Alfred Apsler
Julian Messner, 1973
192 pages, chronology, bibliography, index
    Focusing on de Gaulle's devoted patriotism, this account includes both his strengths and weaknesses. His unpredictability and his caustic style in dealing with people is described. The information about his participation in World War II is not extensive, but the book gives a flavor of his personality, which certainly had some influence during summit meetings.

War Resistance Stories
Written by Arthur Prager and Emily Prager
Illustrated by Steven Assel
Franklin Watts, 1979
90 pages, bibliography, index
    Brief accounts of six men and women in occupied countries who risked and sometimes lost their lives to help others.

Fiction Books

Ceremony of Innocence
Written by James Forman
Hawthorn Books, Inc., 1970
249 pages
    A fictionalized version based on factual information and featuring actual people of the White Rose resistance movement.

The Devil in Vienna
Written by Doris Orgel
Dial Press, 1978
246 pages
    Caught in the strange and frightening events taking place in Vienna in 1938, Jewish Inge Dorenwald and her best friend, Lieselotte Vessely, found it difficult to continue their friendship. As life became more dangerous and frightening for Inge and her family, the friends met only in secret. When Inge's family made

plans to escape, the relationship with Lieselotte became helpful. The story is based on the author's personal experience of escaping from Vienna to Yugoslavia.

The Devil's Arithmetic
Written by Jane Yolen
Viking Kestrel, 1988
170 pages

In this time-slip story, a present-day Jewish girl finds herself in Poland with some of her relatives in the 1940s. She is caught up in the joy of preparing for an uncle's wedding. But the festivities are tragically interrupted by Nazi troops, who herd the Jews into trucks, take all of their jewelry and valuables, and transfer them to boxcars for transportation to the death camps. The horror and routine of the camp is vividly described from the teenage girl's viewpoint.

Displaced Person
Written by Marie Halun Bloch
Lothrop, Lee & Shepard Books, 1978
192 pages

To escape the Red Army, Stefan and his father have traveled from Poltava in the Ukraine to Germany. They find themselves among thousands of other Eastern Europeans who are fleeing from their homes in the final days of the war. Stefan's father has brought a valise containing botanical drawings of plants of the Ukraine that he and Stefan carefully protect. After his father's death, Stefan takes responsibility for getting the precious papers and himself to an American camp.

Don't Say a Word
Written by Barbara Gehrts
Translated from the German by Elizabeth D. Crawford
Margaret K. McElderry Books, Macmillan Publishing Company, 1986
169 pages

The misery of the war for the German people is vividly described in this book based on Gehrts' own childhood. Her father, a high-ranking officer in the Luftwaffe, was opposed to Hitler and sympathetic toward the plight of the Jews. He was arrested on the charge of undermining the war effort and executed four months later. Her brother died from an untreated ear infection while serving in the army. She also suffered the loss of a Jewish friend whose family committed suicide, and a cousin who was killed in action in the war. This engrossing story provides an unusual perspective of the war, not generally found in books written for young people.

Edge of Darkness
Written by Lynne Gessner
Walker and Company, 1979
180 pages

Set in Latvia between June 1941 and October 1944, this story illustrates the terror of living under the rule of first the Russians and then the Germans.

Empire of the Sun
Written by J. G. Ballard
Simon & Schuster, Inc., 1984
375 pages

Relates the story of a British boy who survived Japanese prison camps and other atrocities after being separated from his parents when the war began in China. A vivid account of hunger, suffering, and death.

Goodnight, Mr. Tom
Written by Michelle Magorian
Harper & Row Publishers, 1981
318 pages

As an evacuee from London to the English countryside, young Willie finds love and friendship, which he had not known with his abusive mother. When his mother sends for him to return, he suffers, not only from the effects of the war, but also from his mother's mental illness. Mr. Tom, Willie's country guardian, leaves his comfortable home to search for his young friend.

Hear O Israel: A Story of the Warsaw Ghetto
Written by Terry Walton Treseder
Illustrated by Lloyd Boom
Atheneum, 1990
41 pages

A poignant story told from a young boy's point of view as he tries to understand the changes in his life. His happiness at his older brother's bar mitzvah and his joy in family religious ceremonies is soon shadowed by the building of a wall around the ghetto where he lives. Food becomes scarce, people begin starving to death, and then typhus claims many lives. The boy loses his grandfather, his mother, two sisters, and a brother. Then the trains come to take them to a work camp. The boy, his father, and his older brother are taken to Treblinka.

Hide and Seek
Written by Ida Vos
Translated by Terese Edelstein and Inez Smith
Netherlands: Uitgeverij Leopold, 1981
United States: Houghton Mifflin Company, 1991

Imagine what it would be like to be eight years old and have your world turned inside out, never to be the same again. Vos effectively takes the reader back to Holland in 1940 when the German soldiers invaded and Jewish people were forbidden to carry on any of their normal activities. Then they were forced into hiding. Kind people helped them, but parents were separated from children and Jews went months without stepping outside. When the war was finally over, some family members were reunited, but every Jewish person experienced an overwhelming sense of grief for the many relatives who had died. Written in a terse, episodic format, this account is based on the author's own childhood spent in hiding.

In the Eye of War
Written by Margaret Chang and Raymond Chang
Margaret K. McElderry Books, Macmillan Publishing Company, 1990
198 pages

Based on the author's childhood in Shanghai, this story provides a view of Chinese life and customs as the reality of the war intrudes at an increasing rate. Ten-year-old Shao-shao relates his perception of food and fuel shortages, air raids of American bombers, and his fear of the Japanese soldiers occupying the city. When his father must be smuggled away due to his work with the underground movement, the war takes on a very personal meaning for the whole family.

Island on Bird Street
Written by Uri Orlev
Translated from the Hebrew by Hillel Halkin
Houghton Mifflin Company, 1981
162 pages

After his mother has disappeared and his father has been taken to an unknown destination by the German army, 11-year-old Alex must survive on his own. He lives in a boarded up, abandoned building at 78 Bird Street. Each day he lowers a handmade rope ladder and forages for food and fuel. He manages to survive constant life-threatening circumstances for nine months.

Journey Home
Written by Yoshiko Uchida
Atheneum, 1978
131 pages

Yuki's experiences of surviving in a concentration camp in Utah are vividly described. Yuki's family, Japanese-Americans, have been deported as enemy aliens. When they return home to California after the war, they find their home and belongings are gone. Finding work and a place to live is difficult, and anti-Japanese violence is a constant threat, but Yuki's family manages to make a new beginning.

Journey into War
Written by Margaret Donaldson
Illustrated by Joanna Stuffs
Andre Deutsch, 1979
152 pages

When ten-year-old Janey is accidently stranded in Dunkirk on her way to England in 1940, she joins two Polish boys in declaring their own war on the Germans. They begin their adventures with some success, but soon Janey is captured by the Gestapo, and her newfound friends must find a way to rescue her without becoming prisoners themselves.

The Last Mission
Written by Harry Mazer
Delacorte Press, 1979
182 pages

A 15-year-old boy lies about his age and joins the army. The experiences of war and the difficulties of readjusting to civilian life provide some thought-provoking questions.

Love You, Soldier
Written by Amy Hest
Four Winds Press, 1991
48 pages

A simply told story of a young girl in New York who watches her father leave for war and anxiously waits for his return. She and her mother look forward to his letters, reading and rereading each one. When the uniformed messenger arrives with the news that her father has been killed, Katie and her mother are shocked and sad. They find comfort in sharing their apartment with a friend of Katie's mother and her baby until the end of the war.

The Man from the Other Side
Written by Uri Orlev
Translated from the Hebrew by Hillel Halkin
Houghton Mifflin Company, 1991
186 pages

A vivid picture of life in the Warsaw Ghetto is revealed through the experiences of Marek, a young Polish boy who lives nearby. He helps his stepfather smuggle food into the Ghetto and Jewish babies out through the sewers under the streets. After his mother reveals his true heritage, he befriends a young Jewish man, helping him to hide and eventually leading him back into the Ghetto just before the uprising. Based on the life of a Polish journalist.

Number the Stars
Written by Lois Lowry
Houghton Mifflin Company, 1989
137 pages

This story personalizes the account of the Danish resistance, which managed to smuggle many Jewish people across the sea to Sweden. Annemarie and her family take in her Jewish friend, Ellen Rosen, and pretend she is one of the family, managing to save her life when Nazi soldiers search their home. Then Annemarie is called upon to play an important part in the escape of her friend's family.

Pearl Harbor is Burning! A Story of World War II
(Once Upon America Series)
Written by Kathleen V. Kudlinski
Illustrated by Ronald Himler
Viking, 1991
64 pages

Frank and a friend are in his tree house overlooking Pearl Harbor the morning of 7 December 1941. They watch with fascination and horror as the ships are blown up. Confusion reigns as conflicting messages are heard over the radio about the emergency. This snapshot in historical time presents a realistic picture of the surprise and confusion of that fateful day.

Petros' War
Written by Alki Zei
Translated from the Greek by Edward Fenton
E. P. Dutton, 1972
236 pages

The effects of the war in Greece are realistically related from a young boy's viewpoint. He begins with the pride his family and the Greek people feel as his beloved Uncle Angelos leaves to fight in October 1940. Then the changes come in his life. His mother worries constantly about finding food, while his unemployed father listens to the radio all day, making notes that he apparently delivers to a resistance group. Petros joins a resistance group himself. He writes slogans on walls and marches in demonstrations shouting, Freedom or death. His grandfather's dire warning that things will get worse when the Italians leave and the Germans arrive proves horribly true. The Germans haul people off in bird cages, and they are not seen again. All of the Jewish people are taken and other citizens are picked up at random. Petros has become a young man of 14 by the end of the war.

Rain of Fire
Written by Marion Dane Bauer
Clarion Books, 1983
153 pages

Steve wants Matthew, his brother who has recently returned from fighting in Japan, to be a hero. But Matthew will not talk about his war experiences. Steve's desire to impress his neighborhood pals gets him involved in a war of sorts right at home. When things are at their worst, Matthew tells the group that he is ashamed of having participated in the war and being a part of the army that bombed Hiroshima. Steve begins to understand Matthew's position when he tells him about the suffering and death he witnessed after the bombing, and their old relationship begins to emerge.

Snow Treasure
Written by Marie McSwigan
Illustrated by Mary Reardon
E. P. Dutton, 1942
179 pages

This classic tale of the Norwegian resistance to the German occupation of their country is based on an actual incident of children outwitting the Nazi soldiers and smuggling gold out of Norway. The gold was transported on children's sleds and loaded onto a Norwegian freighter for shipment to the United States in 1940.

Stepping on the Cracks
Written by Mary Downing Hahn
Clarion Books, 1991
216 pages

The effects of the war in the United States are well portrayed in this story about two sixth-grade girls who discover a friend of their brothers hiding in the woods. The girls know their parents would object to them helping a deserter, because both of their brothers are fighting in Europe. When the young man develops pneumonia, they feel they must get help. This engrossing story also deals with the loss of loved ones, understanding class bullies, and the devastating effects of child and wife abuse.

Touch Wood: A Girlhood in Occupied France
Written by Renee Roth-Hano
Four Winds Press, 1988
297 pages
Written in diary form, this story is based on the author's own experiences when she and her two sisters were hidden in a Catholic woman's residence in Normandy to escape persecution in Paris. The girls live in safety until bombings destroy Normandy, and they must survive hunger and illness in the devastated countryside.

Tug of War
Written by Joan Lingard
Lodestar Books, Dutton, 1989
194 pages
Lukas Petersons is a university professor in Latvia and is, therefore, considered dangerous by the invading Russians. He and his family pack a few belongings and join the crush of refugees leaving the country. They travel from Cesis to Gdynia with the retreating German army. Hugo is separated from his family as they are boarding the train. He loses his glasses and is trampled in the crowd. The story then alternates between the hardships suffered by the Petersons as displaced persons in Germany and Hugo's new life with a kind German family. When the war ends, the Petersons finally find a position and place to live in Canada. Astra has kept hope for the past three years that her twin brother is alive, but Hugo has found evidence that indicates his family is dead.

The Upstairs Room
Written by Johanna Reiss
Thomas Y. Crowell, 1972
197 pages
Johanna Reiss was eight years old in 1940 when the Germans invaded Holland. Two years later she and her sister moved in with the Oosterveld family, Gentiles who lived in a remote farmhouse. As Jews, their lives were in danger. Reiss describes their fear as they

hid in a carefully concealed room while soldiers searched the house, but she also relates a sense of the day-to-day life on the farm with its typical ups and downs. Originally written for her own children, the book conveys a sense of joy and optimism.

We Were Not Like Other People
Written by Ephraim Sevela
Translated from the Russian by Antonina W. Bouis
Harper & Row Publishers, 1989
216 pages

Based on Sevela's own childhood in Russia during the war, this is the story of a boy who was forced to survive on his own. Taken from his home to Siberia at the age of 9, he traveled alone, working in factories and on farms until he joined the army when he was 15. The episodes in the boy's life sometimes shift dramatically without transitions, and incidents of violence are graphically described, causing this book to be more appropriate for mature readers.

When Hitler Stole Pink Rabbit
Written and illustrated by Judith Kerr
Coward, 1972
191 pages

Nine-year-old Anna is convinced that it is necessary to have a difficult childhood if one wishes to be famous, but she sees little chance of that for herself. Then her comfortable life in Berlin changes abruptly. Fortunately, her family leaves for Switzerland just before the elections in 1933, because their passports would have been confiscated the next day. Her father finds work in Paris and Anna learns the French language and customs while she also adjusts to being poor. The story ends as her family arrives in England. They anticipate starting all over again, but are happy they continue to be together as refugees. Based on the author's childhood experiences.

Year of Impossible Goodbyes
Written by Sook Nyul Choi
Houghton Mifflin Company, 1991
171 pages

This view of the hardships suffered by people in northern Korea is based on the author's childhood experiences. The story begins with the atrocities inflicted on the Koreans during the Japanese occupation. Ten-year-old Sookan and her younger brother work with their mother and aunt to produce ever increasing quotas of socks in their small factory. Sookan is forced to attend a Japanese school and life becomes almost unbearable. Things seem to be better for a short time after the war. Then the Communists arrive and life becomes a nightmare again. Sookan helps her younger brother escape to South Korea when they become separated from their mother near the border.

Sample Lesson Plan

Introduction

Ask the students what they know about World War II and make a list of their comments on transparencies or chart paper. Then ask what they would like to know and make another list. Save these lists for referral at a later time. Read *Rose Blanche* aloud to the group. Discuss the viewpoint of the child in observing the war in Germany. What did the students discover about the war from sharing this book?

Building Background

Meet in the school library. Divide the students into groups of two or three and look for answers to some of their questions. Look for verification of some of the "facts" students had listed that may or may not have been correct. Ask students to locate and read one library book that gives an overview of World War II or one article in a computer program or encyclopedia. Distribute the glossary list. Ask students to check off terms they come across and add to the definitions as they read.

Meet in small groups of five or six students to share and record facts. Then ask each group to report to the large group. Each small group should contain some students who read encyclopedias and some who read trade books.

Issues

Balance of Power

How had the Treaty of Versailles sown the seeds for another world conflict? Why was the League of Nations ineffective in maintaining world peace? Why had nations grouped themselves into Axis and Allied alliances?

German Aggression

How did other countries in Europe react to the German invasions of Czechoslovakia and Poland? At what point did other countries in the world begin to take note of German aggression? Why had German aggression been allowed to continue unchecked for so long?

The Holocaust

Read *Elie Wiesel: Messenger from the Holocaust* aloud. Discuss Wiesel's personal victory in having survived the Holocaust and the contributions that won him the Nobel Peace Prize.

Read *The Children We Remember* or *The Number on My Grandfather's Arm* aloud. Discuss factual books students have read that describe aspects of the war in Germany and surrounding Axis-controlled countries, such as Poland. Students will need some sensitive direction in thinking about and discussing the horrors of the Holocaust. Consider dividing the class into two smaller groups and having one discussion led by the teacher and the other led by the librarian. A sharing session for the whole group could bring thoughts together during the last part of the class.

Japanese Aggression

Discuss the actions of the Japanese in the Pacific Theater of the war. How did the world react to the Japanese invasions of China and Korea? Why did Japan bomb the American Pacific Fleet in Pearl Harbor? Why did Japan feel that territorial expansion in Asia and the Pacific was necessary?

Major Battles and Turning Points

Topics of discussion may include the Germany blitzkrieg in France, the German invasion of the Soviet Union, the evacuation of British soldiers from Dunkirk, the Battle of Britain, the British and

German offensives in North Africa, the Japanese attack on Pearl Harbor, the Battle of Midway, the Invasion of Normandy, and the dropping of the bombs on Hiroshima and Nagasaki. What was the worldwide reaction to V-E Day and V-J Day?

Political and Military Leadership

Talk about world leaders and their actions in the period between the two world wars. What were some of their concerns and how did they formulate objectives for their countries based on those concerns? How did the role of a head of state in a democracy differ from the role of a head of state in a dictatorship?

Distribute a list of world leaders and ask students to indicate a first, second, and third choice for people they would be interested in researching. Possible names to include are Winston Churchill, Dwight D. Eisenhower, Franklin Delano Roosevelt, Harry Truman, George C. Marshall, Douglas MacArthur, George Patton, Bernard Montgomery, Adolf Hitler, Heinrich Himmler, Erwin Rommell, Sir Alan Brooke, Joseph Stalin, Charles de Gaulle, Omar Bradley, Chiang Kai-shek, Isoruku Yamamoto, Hideki Tojo, and Emperor Hirohito.

Assign students to groups of two, based on their choices. Ask them to prepare a profile of their assigned person, listing dates of birth and death, education, official title, qualifications for that position, major accomplishments, and a statement about how that person is now viewed in history. Compile these profiles into a "World War II Leaders Booklet" and keep it available for reference throughout the rest of the unit.

Projects—World War II Art Show

Share *The Journey* by Sheila Hamanaka with the students. Discuss the ways in which she used murals an an art form to express her feelings. What are some other ways of expressing ideas through art?

Tell students that the culminating activity for this unit will be an art show. Ask each student to be thinking of an art piece that will represent one aspect of the war in a meaningful way. They may create a painting, a collage, a sculpture, a mobile, a diorama, or any other art piece that will convey their message. Perhaps the art teacher or some local artists could visit the class to demonstrate art images and media.

Fiction Books and Biographies

Talk about the ways in which biographies and fiction books can bring life to facts and statistics about the war. Distribute bibliographies of appropriate titles. The countries the stories are set in should be indicated in the bibliography so that students may select stories from different parts of the world. Ask all students to read at least one book, but encourage them to read several. Relevant information may be captured using the reporting forms in Appendix B.

Meet in groups of four or five with each student having read a book set in a different country. Share ways in which the characters' experiences were the same throughout the world. What were some of the regional differences? Meet as a large group and ask students to give brief book talks about titles they would like to recommend to others.

Guidelines for Book Talks

- Read the book. Two readings are even better.
- Show the book or the book jacket.
- Create interest while establishing the setting.
- Describe the most distinctive traits of the main character.
- Use words that evoke emotions.
- Do not tell too much.
- Do not tell the ending.
- End with a "hooker." (A statement designed to pique curiosity and entice listeners to read the book.)

Effects of the War

In Europe

Read aloud *The Angel with a Mouth-Organ* by Christobel Mattingley. Discuss the devastation of European cities and much of the land. Compare the estimated casualties of the Axis and Allied nations. Review the distress of displaced persons with no place to go. How were millions of civilians affected?

In the United States

Read *My Daddy Was a Soldier* aloud. Discuss the effects of the war in the United States. Review reasons for the U.S. entry into the war. How were Japanese-American citizens treated during and after the war? What have been some of the long-term effects of refugees relocating in the United States?

In Japan

Read aloud *Hiroshima No Pika* by Toshi Maruki, *My Hiroshima* by Junko Morimoto, or *Faithful Elephants: A True Story of Animals* by Yukio Tsuchiya. Discuss the immediate and long-range effects of the atomic bomb. What have been some of the changes in Japan since the war?

Overall Effects of the War

Discuss the complexity of the war. What did students learn about events throughout the world? What do they think are the most significant ideas to remember about the unit? Ask students to evaluate the unit. (See Appendix B for an evaluation form.)

Culminating Activity

Prepare an art show displaying the students' art pieces. This may be in a large area in the school, in the district professional library, in a public library, or in a local place of business, such as a bank.

Hold an opening night reception. Invite parents, administrators, school board members, the local media, and the public. Identify student artists with name tags. Ask them to be prepared to talk to guests about their pieces and their study of the war.

Suggested Questions

How did the Paris Peace Conference and the terms of the Treaty of Versailles contribute to the beginning of World War II?

Why was the League of Nations ineffective in maintaining peace?

How might the effectiveness of the League of Nations have differed if the United States, Germany, and the Soviet Union had been members?

How is a dictatorship different from a democracy?

In what ways did the Spanish Civil War influence the rest of Europe?

How did Hitler and Mussolini rise to positions of power?

Why did England's policy of appeasement with Hitler fail?

What characteristics did Hitler envision for the master race?

How did Hitler himself measure up to this criteria?

What were some of the contributions and occupations of Jewish people in Germany prior to the war?

Why didn't the United States government intervene in stopping the atrocities of Nazi concentration camps?

What are some examples of the survival of the human spirit in concentration camps?

Why did some people choose to become part of the resistance movement, even though they knew this would place their lives in danger?

How did the secret war against Hitler contribute to his defeat?

How were people in the Balkan countries victims of the war from both sides?

What effect did the nonagression pact between Germany and the Soviet Union have on Poland?

How did the German army defeat France?

How did the British people react to the German's blitzkrieg warfare?

How did Winston Churchill's leadership contribute to the strength of the English people?

Why did the war spread into Africa?

What factors did Hitler fail to take into account in his invasion of the Soviet Union?

How was the United States involved in the ongoing Battle of the Atlantic even when the country was not officially in the war?

In what ways was Operation Overlord important to the Allies?

What were the results of the Normandy invasion?

Why did the Japanese attack the American Pacific Fleet in Pearl Harbor?

What choices did the United States have after the attack on Pearl Harbor?

What was the Japanese plan for conquest?

What did the vows of kamikaze pilots reveal about Japanese beliefs?

Why did the United States drop two atomic bombs on Japan?

What have been the long-term effects of the dropping of atomic bombs on Japan?

What is Japan's present economic and political status in the world?

How did the war effect a change in women's roles in the United States?

Suggested Activities

Make a chart of the treaties made, the countries that signed them, and their conditions, beginning with the Treaty of Versailles and continuing through 1939.

Make a timeline showing major events in the life of Adolf Hitler.

List some examples of propaganda spread by the Nazi government.

Make a chart comparing Germany's economic status before the war and immediately after the war with its present economic status.

Make a graph comparing the estimated death toll numbers from concentration camps with deaths as a result of the atomic bombs dropped on Japan.

Construct a model of a U-boat.

Present a speech that Winston Churchill could have delivered to the English people during the war.

Make a list of supplies needed in an air raid shelter.

Present a panel discussion on the causes for the Japanese attack on Pearl Harbor and the U.S. reactions to the event.

Prepare a debate on how to deal with Japanese, German, and Italian residents in the United States based on the perceived facts in December 1941.

Write a story that could have been written by a young Japanese-American describing the effects of the war on his/her family.

Make a chart comparing Japan's economic status before the war and immediately after the war with its present economic status.

Record a fireside chat that could have been broadcast by President Franklin D. Roosevelt during the war.

Write a biography of one of the generals who led decisive campaigns during the war.

Research and report on the development of the atomic bomb.

Create a poster encouraging people to plant victory gardens.

Create a picture book illustrating a variety of propaganda techniques.

Create a chart showing jobs held by women during the war.

Present a panel discussion about the war with students taking the parts of Sir Winston Churchill, Franklin D. Roosevelt, Charles de Gaulle, and Joseph Stalin.

Glossary

Allied nations—Countries joined in the fight against the Axis nations of Germany, Italy, and Japan. Original Allies were Great Britain, France, Canada, Australia, New Zealand, and South Africa. The United States and the Soviet Union joined later.

amphibious landing—Military forces arriving in ships and walking through water to get to land.

appeasement—The belief that war could be prevented by meeting Hitler's demands.

Atlantic Charter—A statement of postwar aims of Great Britain and the United States issued in 1941.

Axis nations—Germany, Italy, and Japan.

blitzkrieg (blitz)—War waged with great speed and force; literally "lightning war."

concentration camp—Prison camp supervised by the SS, where Nazis sent people declared to be dangerous to Nazi-controlled countries.

Crystal Night—The night of 9 November 1938, when throughout Germany people shattered the glass windows of Jewish shops, synagogues, and homes.

death camp—A camp built with the express purpose of killing Jewish people and other political prisoners.

displaced persons—People left without homes as a result of the war. Many were survivors of concentration or war camps. Others fled their homes because of invading armies.

enemy aliens—A classification given to more than a million newly arrived immigrants to the United States from Germany, Italy, and Japan during the war. The Japanese were relocated in inland concentration camps.

final solution—A term used by Hitler and the Nazis for elimination of the Jewish people.

genocide—The deliberate destruction of a racial, political, or cultural group; a combination of the Greek word *genos* (meaning race, tribe, or group) and the Latin word *cide* (meaning kill).

Gestapo—Hitler's secret police force, which ruthlessly crushed opposition to the Nazi party.

ghetto—A part of the city, often surrounded by walls or fences, in which Jewish people were required to live.

GI—A slang term for American soldiers, meaning "government issue."

government rationing—A system established for distribution of scarce goods.

Hitler Youth—Nazi groups organized to indoctrinate the young people of Germany with party-line goals and loyalties.

holocaust—A great raging fire that consumes all in its path; the largest loss of life ever suffered by one peopleEuropean Jewsduring World War II.

judenfrage—The theory that the entire Jewish race must be eliminated.

kamikaze—A corps of Japanese pilots prepared to die in order to destroy enemy warships, transports, or other targets.

lebensraum—The belief that Germany needed more land and was entitled to invade her neighbors to acquire it.

Lend-Lease Act—Permitted President Roosevelt to lend or lease raw materials, equipment, and weapons to any nation fighting the Axis powers.

mischlinge—Person of mixed Jewish and Aryan backgrounds; subjected to the same treatment as full-blooded Jews.

Nazi party—Hitler's political party, shortened from National Sozialistche Deutsche Arbeiterpartei (National Socialist German Workers' party).

neutral nations—Sweden, Switzerland. These countries did not join sides with either the Axis nations or the Allies.

Nuremberg Laws—German laws of 15 September 1935, the most significant of which stated that Jews could no longer be German citizens. They were forbidden to fly the German flag, to attend German schools, or to own property or businesses.

Nuremberg Trials—Trials held after the war (from 1945 to 1949) for people accused of crimes during the war.

Operation Overlord—The code name for the Allied plan to invade Europe by crossing from England into France; this took place on D-Day, 6 June 1944.

pogrom—A surprise attack against a defenseless Jewish community.

propaganda—Information released by a government to influence public opinion.

psychological warfare—Misleading information intended to destroy the enemy's will to fight.

refugee—A person left homeless as a result of the war.

resistance group—People working underground to oppose the government, often helping Jewish people to escape to neutral or Allied countries.

SS—Schutzstaffel; Hitler's special security force. Also called Blackshirts.

swastika—An ancient religious symbol adapted and used as the symbol of the Nazi party in 1920.

Third Reich—The official name of the Nazi party, meaning the third empire. The First Reich was the Holy Roman Empire in the Middle Ages. The Second Reich was Germany's unification under the rule of Prussia, 1871–1918.

Ultra—England's breaking of the German code for secret messages, allowing the Allies to intercept vital military information.

underground—A secret movement to resist the powers of an occupying government.

Zionism—A movement to establish Palestine (now Israel) as the national Jewish homeland.

Vietnam War Literature Unit

Selected Chronology

1945	September 2	Ho Chi Minh issued a proclamation of independence as the Japanese surrendered and World War II was over. The proclamation was not recognized by any major power.
1946		Signing of the Franco-Vietnamese (preliminary) accords by Ho Chi Minh and Jean Sainteny of France.
	July–August	Fontainebleau Conference.
	December 19	The Vietnamese war for independence against France began.
1950		The United States agreed to supply arms to the French in their war against Ho Chi Minh's Vietminh.
1951		The United States signed an agreement to provide direct military and economic aid to the government of South Vietnam.
1952		The United States was paying for as much as one-half of the French war effort.
1953	January	Dwight D. Eisenhower became president of the United States.
		The Vietminh challenged French troops in Laos.
1954	May	Defeat of the French army at Dien Bien Phu.
	July	Geneva Accords specified that Vietnam would be temporarily divided into two zones (north and south) pending a referendum to be held in 1956.
		Ngo Dinh Diem became prime minister of South Vietnam.
		The Southeast Asia Treaty Organization (SEATO) was formed.
		The last French forces left Hanoi.
		China agreed to provide aid and equipment to Hanoi
1955		Ho Chi Minh traveled to Moscow and received Soviet support for his unification program.

	October	Diem proclaimed himself president of the Republic of Vietnam.
		The United States began sending aid to South Vietnam.
1956		President Ngo Dinh Diem refused to hold elections, as had been specified in the Geneva agreement.
		All French troops were withdrawn from Vietnam.
1957		Communist insurgency activities killed more than 400 government officials in South Vietnam.
		Communist guerrilla activities began in South Vietnam.
1958		Communists established a command structure in the Mekong Delta region.
		North Vietnamese soldiers began to invade South Vietnam.
1959		Two American soldiers were killed at Bien Hoa.
1960		Hanoi formed the National Liberation Front (NLF) to serve as the governing body of the Vietcong in South Vietnam.
1961	January	John F. Kennedy became president of the United States.
		Vice President Johnson visited Vietnam and advocated aid to its government.
		Four hundred Special Forces troops and 100 other advisors were sent to Vietnam.
1962		Major buildup of U.S. advisors in Vietnam.
1963	May	President Diem prohibited the flying of the Buddhist flag, resulting in widespread dissent among Buddhists in major Vietnamese cities.
	November	President Diem was overthrown and killed.
	November	Lyndon B. Johnson became president of the United States when John F. Kennedy was assassinated.
1964	August 7	The Gulf of Tonkin Resolution granted President Johnson special powers to act in Southeast Asia following the report of an attack on an American destroyer.
		U Thant's diplomatic initiatives were accepted by Hanoi but rejected by Washington
1965	February	U.S. bombers attacked North Vietnam in retaliation for a Vietcong raid on the helicopter port at Plei Ku.
	March	The first American combat troops were sent to South Vietnam.

	June	Nguyen Coa Ky was named premier of South Vietnam as head of a ten-man military junta.
	August	First major American victory at Chu Lai.
		Antiwar teach-ins were held on college and university campuses throughout the United States.
		By the end of the year, U.S. troop strength in Vietnam numbered 200,000.
1966	March	Lieutenant General Nguyen Chanh Thi was dismissed, causing widespread protests and rioting in South Vietnam.
	June	U.S. bombers began attacking near Hanoi and Haiphong.
		The Senate Foreign Relations Committee began questioning presidential advisors about U.S. involvement in the war.
1967		Villagers thought to be sympathetic to the Vietcong were relocated in refugee camps, and their villages destroyed.
		General Nguyen Van Thieu was elected president of South Vietnam.
		Antiwar demonstrations took place throughout the United States.
		The number of U.S. forces in Vietnam reached nearly 500,000.
1968	January–February	North Vietnamese and the Vietcong attacked most of the major cities and military bases in South Vietnam during the Tet Offensive.
		The My Lai massacre destroyed a village of between 200 and 600 Vietnamese civilians.
	March 31	President Johnson ordered a limited halt to the bombing and requested a peace conference.
	May	Formal peace talks began in Paris.
	November	A full bombing halt began.
		A total of 540,000 Americans were in Vietnam.
1969	January	Richard M. Nixon became president of the United States.
		Secret bombing of Cambodia began.
	June 8	President Nixon announced the policy of Vietnamization, which provided increased training for South Vietnamese forces and gradual withdrawal of U.S. troops.
	September 3	Ho Chi Minh died at the age of 79.
		Antiwar rallies were held in Washington, D.C.

		The number of U.S. troops in South Vietnam dropped to 480,000.
1970		Air attacks on North Vietnam were resumed.
	April	American and South Vietnamese forces invaded Cambodia.
	May 4	National Guardsmen killed 4 students and wounded 11 others at an antiwar demonstration at Kent State University in Ohio.
		The number of U.S. troops in Vietnam fell to 280,000.
1971		Congress repealed the Gulf of Tonkin Resolution.
	March	Lieutenant William Calley was convicted of murder in connection with the massacre at My Lai.
	June	Newspapers published the Pentagon Papers.
		U.S. forces in Vietnam totaled 140,000.
1972	March	North Vietnam began a major invasion of South Vietnam.
	April	President Nixon increased the bombing of North Vietnam.
	October	A tentative peace agreement was reached through secret meetings of representatives from the United States and North Vietnam, but Saigon objected to the terms and it was not signed.
		U.S. combat troops numbered fewer than 30,000.
1973	January 27	A cease-fire agreement was signed in Paris.
	March 29	All American troops were withdrawn.
	August	The Senate voted to forbid aid to Vietnam without congressional approval.
		War Powers Act passed by Congress.
1974	August 9	Richard M. Nixon resigned as president of the United States and Gerald Ford became president.
1975	March	The North Vietnamese forced South Vietnamese troops to retreat from the central highlands.
		Cambodia, Laos, and Saigon fell to the communists.
	April 30	South Vietnam surrendered to North Vietnam in Saigon, which was renamed Ho Chi Minh City.
1976		The two Vietnams were officially reunified.
1977	January	James Earl Carter became president of the United States.
		President Carter pardoned 10,000 draft evaders.
		Vietnamese refugees began to flee the country.
1982		The Vietnam Veterans Memorial was dedicated in Washington, D.C.

Recommended Books

Picture Books

Angel Child, Dragon Child
Written by Michele Maria Surat
Illustrated by Vo-Dinh Mai
Scholastic, Inc., 1983
36 pages

The confusion and fear of starting in a new school in a new land is well presented through the eyes of Ut, the youngest daughter of a Vietnamese family recently immigrated to the United States. The teasing and cruelty of her classmates gives way to concern and help when they find out that Ut's mother is still in Vietnam waiting for the family to earn enough money for her to join them. The students organize and conduct a Vietnamese Fair fund-raiser to help out.

Lee Ann: The Story of a Vietnamese-American Girl
Written by Tricia Brown
Illustrated with black-and-white photographs by Ted Thai
G. P. Putnam's Sons, 1991
48 pages

Presented in a photo-documentary format, this is the story of a young Vietnamese girl who was born in a refugee camp while her parents waited for permission to immigrate to the United States. She tells about her life in America and then describes the traditional Vietnamese food and customs that are still honored in her home. Celebration of the Tet holiday is featured.

The Wall
Written by Eve Bunting
Illustrated by Ronald Himler
Clarion Books, 1990
32 pages

A young boy and his father come to the Vietnam Veterans Memorial in Washington, D.C., to find the name of the boy's grandfather. He observes other people looking for the names of their loved ones who died in the war while his father makes a rubbing of his grandfather's name. Although the boy and his father discuss the pride they feel, their sense of loss is poignantly felt.

Factual Books

An Album of the Vietnam War
Written by Don Lawson
Illustrated with black-and-white photographs
Franklin Watts, 1986
88 pages, maps, index

Begins with the close of World War II and France's concern over its diminished colonial empire, which resulted in that country's opposition to the Vietnamese people's struggle for independence. The gradual involvement of the United States and the events that influenced the presidents and military leaders of the time are explained in a straightforward manner.

Always To Remember:
The Story of the Vietnam Veterans Memorial
Written by Brent Ashabranner
Illustrated with black-and-white photographs by Jennifer Ashabranner
Dodd, Mead & Company, 1988
100 pages, bibliography, index

A brief summary of the war is followed by a description of Jan Scruggs' vision of a memorial featuring the names of all those who died in Vietnam. Support for the project came from congressmen, veterans, and citizens who envisioned the memorial as a symbol to promote healing of the country's wounds by honoring the fallen warriors. The choice of Maya Lin's design and details of the construction are included. Accounts of some of the visitors and mementos that are left at the wall provide a sense of the healing that is taking place.

America and Vietnam: The Elephant and the Tiger
Written by Albert Marrin
Illustrated with black-and-white photographs
Viking, 1992
277 pages, bibliography, index

Vietnamese yearning for independence and hatred of invaders can be traced to 111 B.C. when Vietnam was conquered by China. Marrin has dealt with the complexities of this history and the U.S. involvement in a sensitive way. His main premise is based on a Ho Chi Minh quote which compares the Vietnamese to a tiger that never pauses in its pursuit of the larger elephant until it dies of exhaustion and loss of blood. The exploitation of the country by the French serves as a background for the Vietnamese people's admiration of Ho Chi Minh. The escalation of the war by Presidents Kennedy and Johnson is attributed to an underestimation of the Vietnamese based on a blend of arrogance and ignorance. The horrors of jungle warfare for U.S. foot soldiers are described. The Tet Offensive, war protests at home, and the failure of President Nixon's Vietnamization plan contribute further to the complexity of the situation. Problems suffered by Vietnam veterans began with angry receptions on their homecomings and continue to haunt their lives as they pay the price for an unpopular war. The closing paragraphs suggest that wisdom can come out of tragedy.

The American Experience in Vietnam
Written by Clark Dougan, Stephen Weiss, and the editors of Boston Publishing Company
Illustrated with color and black-and-white photographs
W. W. Norton & Company and Boston Publishing Company, 1988
352 pages, bibliography

Each of the eight chapters features a summary of an aspect of the war, one or two sections describing a specific event, and one or two eyewitness reports from people who were involved. An attempt to provide a complete history in one volume, this oversize book provides a wide range of factual information.

The American Experience in Vietnam: A Reader
Edited by Grace Sevy
University of Oklahoma Press, 1989
319 pages, index, notes on contributors

A collection of articles and essays related to five topics: American Policy in Vietnam: Why Did We Get In? Why Did We Stay So Long?, A Different War: The Military in Vietnam, The Role of the Press: Was the Coverage of the War Fair?, The Antiwar Movement: Why Was There So Much Opposition?, and The Continuing Controversy: Coming to Terms with a Confusing War. This is a good resource for teachers or for students interested in an in-depth study of one of these topics.

America's Vietnam War: A Narrative History
Written by Elizabeth Becker
Clarion Books, 1992
211 pages, bibliography, index

Based on the Pentagon Papers, first-person accounts, and scholarly studies, this is an objective account of the role of the United States in the affairs of this small country for over 25 years. The complex history of warfare in Vietnam provides perspective for understanding the leaders and political environment. The reasons for the gradual involvement of the U.S. and significant decisions made by Presidents Eisenhower, Kennedy, Johnson, and Nixon are examined along with the changing attitudes about the war among U.S. citizens. A thoughtful, readable contribution to the literature.

Battles and Campaigns in Vietnam 1954–1984
Written by Tom Carhart
Illustrated with black-and-white and color photographs
The Military Press, Crown Publishers, Inc., 1984
191 pages, index

This large format book is profusely illustrated with on-the-scene photographs, beginning with the French defeat at Dien Bien Phu. The chopper war, air war, naval war, and major battles and invasions throughout Vietnam, Cambodia, and Laos are included. The book closes with a description of the never-ending war as Indochina smolders on.

Dear America: Letters Home from Vietnam
Edited by Bernard Edelman for the New York Vietnam Veterans Memorial
  Commission
Foreword by William Broyles, Jr.
Pocket Books, 1985
316 pages, map, glossary, index

Excerpts from letters written by GIs, along with the introduction to the book and introductory notes for each of the eight chapters, express the horror, fear, and frustration of the war. The reader experiences a tour of duty as letters are organized chronologically based on a one-year tour of duty, including arrival in Vietnam, fighting, injuries, premonitions of death, and anticipation of returning home. Several men chose to express their feelings in poetry, providing vivid images of their experiences. About one-third of the letters were written by soldiers who died in Vietnam.

Fighters, Refugees, Immigrants: A Story of the Hmong
Written by Mace Goldfarb, M.D.
Illustrated with color photographs
Carolrhoda Books, Inc., 1982
40 pages

The Hmong were allies of the United States during the war and found it necessary to leave Laos when the communists took over. This book gives a brief glimpse of Ban Vinai, a refugee camp in Thailand, as observed by a pediatrician who went there to help survivors. It portrays a sense of the importance of family and the optimism that permeated the camp in spite of poverty and disease.

Images of War: A Vietnam Portfolio
(The Vietnam Experience Series)
Written by Robert Stone
Illustrated with black-and-white photographs
Boston Publishing Company, 1986
192 pages

Each of the six chapters in this oversize book begins with one page of condensed, intense prose about an aspect of the war, followed by several pages of related photographs. Based on the image of a shattered mirror, the author and photographic staff have presented a kaleidoscope of stark images of the many faces of the war. Graphic pictures of the massive destruction of the country, dead and dying civilians and soldiers, antiwar demonstrations in the United States, and the war's lingering aftermath present a vivid sense of the war experience.

MIA: Missing in Action, A Vietnam Drama
Written by Edward F. Dolan
Franklin Watts, 1989
128 pages, bibliography, index

At the time this book was written, 2,410 Americans were missing in Southeast Asia. The author examines the official government policy stating that they are presumed dead, the conflicting evidence concerning possible sightings, and some of the inconsistencies in information provided to families of MIAs.

No More Vietnams
Written by Richard Nixon
Arbor House, 1985
240 pages

Nixon has presented an interesting view of the war from his perspective. He dismisses many of the facts of the war as myths perpetuated by communist propaganda and irresponsible reporting by the American press. He gives examples of news stories that were distorted and exaggerated, focusing on shortcomings or mistakes of the United States and South Vietnamese, while ignoring atrocities of the Vietcong and North Vietnamese. Congress is blamed for losing the peace after the United States had won the war.

Planning a Tragedy: The Americanization of the War in Vietnam
Written by Larry Berman
W. W. Norton & Company, 1982
203 pages, bibliography, index

Berman has examined the decision-making process that began early in 1965 and intensified during the summer, resulting in the historic decision in July of that year that led to the increased involvement of the United States in the Vietnam War. Relying mainly on primary source documents, the text provides a descriptive narrative of the decision-making process. President Johnson's domineering personality and his need for control in policy sessions is revealed in quotations from memos, letters, and transcripts of discussions. Extensive notes and appendixes document the material presented.

Portrait of a Tragedy: America and the Vietnam War
Written by James A. Warren
Illustrated with black-and-white photographs
Lothrop, Lee & Shepard Books, 1990
207 pages, maps, chronology, bibliography, index

Beginning with the close of World War II and the U.S. decision to support France in reclaiming its colonial territories, this book provides an objective account of the factors that contributed to U.S. involvement and eventual defeat in this conflict. Theories responsible for the escalation of the war and important decisions made during each presidential administration are placed in historical context. Congressional disagreement and antiwar demonstrations are included. The complexity of the issues and the lack of understanding of important cultural differences are emphasized.

The Tet Offensive
Written by Charles Wills
Illustrated with black-and-white and color photographs
Silver Burdett, 1989
64 pages, maps, bibliography, index

The three-page introduction describes the Tet Offensive and sets the stage for showing how a military victory for the United States became a psychological victory for the communists. Most of the remainder of the book summarizes the major events of the war. An afterword discusses the building and dedication of the Vietnam Veterans Memorial in Washington, D.C., and the healing effect it has had for the nation.

Tim Page's Nam
Written by Tim Page
Illustrated with color photographs
Borzoi Books, Alfred A. Knopf, 1983
120 pages

Outstanding full-color photographs taken on location during the war occupy most of the book. A brief commentary accompanies pictures of helicopters and other aircraft, soldiers, marches, and the tragic aftermath of battles. The events portrayed and the language of the text are intended for an adult audience, making this book more appropriate for older and mature students.

The United States in the Vietnam War
Written by Don Lawson
Illustrated with black-and-white photographs
Thomas Y. Crowell, 1981
150 pages, map, bibliography, index

An objective account of the causes of the war, including political, social, economic, and military aspects as the war escalated. Antiwar demonstrations and the increasing commitment of the five American presidents involved in the war are included. The last chapter discusses the continuing aftermath of the war.

Vietnam
(Enchantment of the World Series)
Written by David K. Wright
Illustrated with black-and-white and color photographs
Children's Press, 1989
128 pages, maps, index

Three of the eleven chapters of this book deal with the war. The shift of the fighting from the French to the Americans is covered, and then the ten years of war, including long-term hardships, are discussed. Other chapters describe the geography of the country, life-styles, religion, philosophy, and culture. Famous Vietnamese and a picture tour are included.

Vietnam: There and Here
Written by Margot C. J. Mabie
Illustrated with black-and-white photographs
Holt, Rinehart and Winston, 1985
166 pages, map, glossary, bibliography, index

Focusing on the need for understanding the complexities of the war, this book was written for a generation of young people who were born after 1973 and are confused by the many questions that have no easy answers. Brief historical information is provided as a background. The controversial issues of the war, both in Vietnam and in the United States, are objectively discussed.

The Vietnam War
Written by Richard Edwards
Illustrated with black-and-white photographs
Rourke Enterprises, Inc., 1986
77 pages, glossary, index

Summarizes the major causes and events of the war, beginning with the Gulf of Tonkin confrontation in 1964, and then describes the nationalist heritage of the Vietnamese people. The extent of the destruction of both the land and the people of Vietnam is vividly described. Reasons for the involvement and eventual withdrawal of the United States are included. A summary of the aftermath of the war presents some of its long-term effects.

The Vietnam War
(An Eyewitness History)
Written by Sanford Wexler
Illustrated with black-and-white photographs
Facts on File, 1992
393 pages, maps, chronology, glossary, bibliography, index

This oversize volume contains 12 chapters of detailed information about all aspects of the war. Each chapter includes an introductory essay, a chronology, and first-hand accounts of the war excerpted from memoirs, television reports, speeches, letters, and newspapers. A wide spectrum of opinions and perspectives is supplied through testimonies from American and Vietnamese leaders, military personnel (foot soldiers and officers), nurses, peace protestors, USO performers, and journalists.

The Vietnam War: An Impact Book
Written by E. B. Fincher
Illustrated with black-and-white photographs
Franklin Watts, 1980
87 pages, maps, bibliography, index

The issues and background of the war are placed in historical perspective in an attempt to help readers understand the complexities faced by decision makers of the time. Referring to the conflict as The Quicksand War, Fincher describes the step-by-step involvement that began in 1950, when President Truman sent a military advisory team to aid the French. The war gradually escalated over the years as each succeeding president increased American involvement. The concluding chapter discusses the long-term effects of the war for Vietnam and other nearby countries.

War in Vietnam: Book I—Eve of Battle
Written by David K. Wright
Illustrated with black-and-white photographs
Children's Press, 1989
144 pages, maps, chronology, glossary, index

Wright, a Vietnam veteran, describes the historical tradition of the Vietnamese people's desire for independence. The French-Indochina War and America's increasing involvement in Vietnam are explained. Biographical inserts provide valuable information about some of the key decision makers and influential people of the 1945 to 1965 era. A Timeline of Vietnam: 3000 B.C. to 1988" is included.

War in Vietnam: Book II—A Wider War
Written by David K. Wright
Illustrated with black-and-white photographs
Children's Press, 1989
144 pages, maps, chronology, glossary, index
    Beginning with Lyndon Johnson's presidency in 1963 and con-tinuing through the Tet Offensive in 1968, this book reveals the futility of the war. The frustration of the Americans with Vietnam-ese superstitions and political corruption intensified as the crucial war for the hearts and minds of the local people was being lost. Descriptions of aircraft and bombs reveal the force of power that was used. Antiwar demonstrations in the United States exemplify the lack of total support for the war.

War in Vietnam: Book III—Vietnamization
Written by David K. Wright
Illustrated with black-and-white photographs
Children's Press, 1989
144 pages, maps, chronology, glossary, index
    This account begins with the My Lai 4 massacre and continues with the events related to the war during Richard Nixon's presi-dency. Atrocities committed by both sides are described, and the horror of the border wars in Cambodia and Laos are discussed. Conditions of the cease-fire agreed to in January 1973 conclude the book.

War in Vietnam: Book IV—Fall of Vietnam
Written by David K. Wright
Illustrated with black-and-white photographs
Children's Press, 1989
144 pages, maps, chronology, glossary, index
    The major events following the signing of the peace treaty in 1973 are discussed, beginning with the Watergate scandal and Richard Nixon's resignation. The fall of Saigon and the takeover of neighboring countries by the communists caused thousands of panicked people to flee their countries. Problems of the refugees and of Amerasian youth are realistically described. Some of the

problems of veterans in the United States and the lingering effects of physical and psychological injuries are discussed.

Why We Were in Vietnam
Written by Norman Podhoretz
Simon & Schuster, Inc., 1982
240 pages, index

This scholarly analysis of the participation of the United States in the Vietnam War presents a balanced discussion based on the political structure and beliefs of the time. Arguments ranging from political idealism to political recklessness are examined in a straightforward manner. Recommended for mature students who have a serious interest in exploring the underlying reasons for the war.

Biographies

Dust of Life
Written by Liz Thomas
Insert of black-and-white photographs
E. P. Dutton, 1978
210 pages

When Thomas was 19, she got her first position in a Vietnamese orphanage in Saigon. From 1972 to 1975 she worked in Vietnamese hospitals, visited prisons, founded a home for girls, and was totally involved with the lives of the street people. Her descriptions of the poverty and filth of the city are graphic. Homes, hospitals, and streets were filled with rubbish, infested with rats and insects, and saturated with a suffocating stench. Thomas constantly expresses her love of the people and her desire to be one of them, wearing their traditional clothing, eating the common food, and sharing their afflictions.

Everett Alvarez, Jr.: A Hero for Our Times
(Picture-Story Biographies Series)
Written by Susan Maloney Clinton
Illustrated with black-and-white photographs
Children's Press, 1990
32 pages, index

Alvarez, one of the first prisoners of war, was shot down on 5 August 1964. Some of his horrible experiences, such as being served inedible food and fighting cockroaches in the water, are described. He returned to the United States in 1973 and continued his education in the Navy. After retiring, he was an administrator in the Peace Corps and in the Veterans Administration and a presidential adviser.

Henry Kissinger
(World Leaders: Past & Present Series)
Written by Fred L. Israel
Illustrated with black-and-white photographs
Chelsea House Publishers, 1986
116 pages, chronology, bibliography, index

Recognized as one of the world's finest diplomats, Kissinger received the Nobel Peace Prize for his efforts to bring peace to Vietnam. He tried to return the prize when the North Vietnamese invaded Saigon. Kissinger never discussed his childhood, so all that is known is that he and his family fled Nazi Germany in 1938 and settled in the United States. He graduatedfrom Harvard University and returned there for his doctorate, later becoming a professor at the university. He advised President Eisenhower on foreign policy and became President Nixon's assistant for national security and then his secretary of state. Much of the book is devoted to the war in Vietnam and Kissinger's negotiations for peace.

Ho Chi Minh: A Political Biography
Written by Jean Lacouture
Originally published in French, Editions du Seuil, 1967
Translated from the French by Peter Wiles
Translation edited by Jane Clark Seitz
Random House, 1968
314 pages, chronology, index

This comprehensive biography begins with the sketchy information known about Ho's childhood, expands into his foreign travels, and discusses the development of his adherence to communism. His reputation as a revolutionary and devout nationalist seems to be in contrast to the image of revered uncle, which he projected among the common people. Ho's desire for a united Vietnam and his willingness to seek a peaceful settlement with the French and later with the United States is emphasized.

Ho Chi Minh: Legend of Hanoi

Written by Jules Archer
Crowell-Collier Press, 1971
199 pages, bibliography, index

As a legend in his own time, Ho Chi Minh was universally loved by the people of Vietnam. His entire life was dedicated to his dream of gaining freedom and independence for the Vietnamese. The roots of his revolt against colonialism are traced to his early childhood and the influence of his parents, who actively opposed the French occupation of their country. An extremely intelligent man, he was basically self-educated. Traveling throughout the world, he became conversant in at least ten languages and read classics from all cultures, including the writings of Karl Marx, which deeply influenced his beliefs. Conflicts with France and later the United States are shown through Ho's eyes as he continued to pursue his goal to liberate the people of South Vietnam.

Ho Chi Minh and His Vietnam: A Personal Memoir

Written by Jean Sainteny
Originally published in French as Face a Ho Chi Minh,
    Editions Seghers, 1970
Translated from the French by Herma Briffault
Insert of black-and-white photographs
Cowles Book Company, Inc., 1972
193 pages, index

As the major French diplomat who dealt with Ho Chi Minh from 1945 until his death in 1969, Sainteny presents a compassionate view of the leader of the Democratic Republic of North Vietnam. He summarizes Ho's early travels and studies in France, England, and Russia, emphasizing Ho's consistent and major goal in life: the unification and self-determination of Vietnam as a country. Sainteny expresses sorrow that the Accords of 6 March 1946 did not lead to the eventual decolonization of Vietnam during the Fontainebleau Peace Negotiations as both he and Ho had hoped. Ho's willingness to reach a peaceful agreement and his desire to maintain diplomatic relations with France is the major theme. Also included are Last Will and Testament of President Ho Chi Minh, Funeral Oration at the Memorial Service for Ho Chi Minh, and Chronology of Important Events that Affected the Modern History of Vietnam.

John F. Kennedy: Thirty-Fifth President of the United States
(Encyclopedia of Presidents Series)
Written by Zachary Kent
Illustrated with black-and-white photographs
Children's Press, 1987
100 pages, chronology, index

Although the book begins with Kennedy's heroic rescue of crew members from his wrecked patrol boat during World War II and later describes his strong stand during the Cuban missile crisis, the war in Vietnam is not mentioned in this biography. Kennedy is presented as a likeable young man who lived in his older brother's shadow throughout his childhood and yielded to his father's demand that he become a politician when Joe, Jr. died in the war. Although basically shy, he was a good campaigner and was aided in his elections to Congress and the presidency by his father's money and his large family's commitment.

John F. Kennedy: Young People's President
Written by Catherine Corley Anderson
Illustrated with black-and-white photographs
Lerner Publications Company, 1991
144 pages, bibliography, index

This account presents Kennedy as a personable young man who suffered from a variety of illnesses as a child and chronic back pain as an adult. His heroism in World War II is noted. He graduated with distinction from Harvard University and traveled widely throughout Europe. He followed his father's wishes that he enter politics and served as both a representative and a senator from Massachusetts, before being elected president. Throughout his political life, he showed concern for the poor and underprivileged of the nation and the world. He supported civil rights legislation and created the Peace Corps by executive order. His problems with Cuba and meetings with Soviet Premier Nikita Khruschev are highlighted, as are his successful visits to foreign countries. His involvement in Vietnam is dismissed in a few paragraphs stating that he had inherited the commitment to support a military presence in Vietnam but planned to get the U.S. out of the country during his second term. The shock of his assassination and the nation's grief are well portrayed.

The Land I Lost: Adventures of a Boy in Vietnam
Written by Huynh Quang Nhuong
Illustrated by Vo-Dinh Mai
Harper & Row Publishers, 1982
115 pages

The dangers of life in the central highlands of Vietnam were numerous, including poisonous snakes, wild pigs, and man-eating crocodiles. But the spirit of community and the sense of family caring shines through in these memoirs of childhood. This book provides a vivid sense of what life was like before the war. A glimpse of the impending change is given at the end when the family's faithful water buffalo, Tank, is killed by a stray bullet during a battle of the resistance forces against the French.

Lyndon Baines Johnson, President
Written by John Devaney
Illustrated with black-and-white photographs
Walker and Company, 1986
122 pages, index

Although this is a rather comprehensive view of Johnson's life, it does not focus on his decision-making responsibilities during the war. Reading the book will provide a sense of the kind of man Johnson was and his use of power in public office. The last chapter discusses the war in terms of Johnson's decision not to run for a second term as president.

The President from Texas: Lyndon Baines Johnson
Written by Dudley Lynch
Insert of black-and-white photographs
Thomas Y. Crowell, 1975
169 pages, bibliography, index

This biography covers all of Johnson's life, but the last four chapters specifically deal with the crushed dreams of his presidency due to the Vietnam War conflict. From the moment Lyndon Johnson was sworn in as president of the United States, he began dealing with the Vietnam problem. His escalation of the war while trying to create the Great Society at home caused him to leave the White House in defeat.

Richard Nixon: A Political Life
Written by Richard M. Pious
Illustrated with black-and-white photographs
Julian Messner, 1991
113 pages, chronology, bibliography, index

Nixon is presented as an ambitious man, involved in politics throughout his life. He used questionable, if not dishonest, tactics in all of his campaigns for office and rose to fame through his persistent pursuit of Communists on the House Committee on Un-American Activities. His strength was in foreign relations. He is credited with bringing an end to the Vietnam War, as well as with opening diplomatic channels with China and the Soviet Union. Nixon's implication in the Watergate break-in and his resignation from office are described. The author concludes that "Nixon the statesman was tarnished by Nixon the politician."

Richard M. Nixon, President
(Presidential Biography Series)
Written by Sallie G. Randolph
Illustrated with black-and-white photographs
Walker and Company, 1989
136 pages, index

A balanced view of this controversial president is presented. His childhood in California and his early political career are covered. Establishing diplomatic ties with China and bringing an end to the war in Vietnam are listed among his successes in office. His decisions concerning the war are not discussed in any detail.

Fiction Books

And One for All
Written by Theresa Nelson
Orchard Books, 1989
182 pages

The statistics of the war come vividly to life in this story of a teenage girl who loses her brother, Wing, in Vietnam. The complexity of issues is well presented. Geraldine's father is a veteran of World War II and considers war protesters to be traitors to the country. Wing's best friend, Sam, has become an active war protestor. Frequent reports of television news broadcasts lend immediacy to the story.

The Best of Friends
Written by Margaret I. Rostkowski
Harper & Row Publishers, 1989
183 pages

The Vietnam War serves as a backdrop for this story of changing relationships among three teenagers. Dan and Will have been friends throughout their school years. As graduation gets closer, Will begins to question his constant reliance on Dan's judgment and notices that Dan's younger sister, Sarah, is interesting in her own right. The young people deal with the war in individual ways. Sarah becomes active in the antiwar movement, despite their father's firm support of the war, as exemplified by his position as head of the local draft board. Dan rips his draft card in half in defiance of his autocratic father. Will enlists in the army on graduation day.

Charlie Pippin
Written by Candy Dawson Boyd
Macmillan Publishing Company, 1987
182 pages

Chartreuse (Charlie) Pippin, a spunky sixth-grader in Berkeley, California, cannot understand why her father will not talk to her about his experiences in Vietnam. Her father is opposed to her participation in a war and peace project for school and refuses to be interviewed. As Charlie conducts her research and attends a peace demonstration with her grandmother, she learns that her father's dreams had been shattered as a result of the war.

December Stillness
Written by Mary Downing Hahn
Clarion Books, 1988
181 pages

Kelly decides to write her contemporary issue paper on the homeless and to use a troubled Vietnam veteran who frequents the library as her subject. Mr. Weems is not interested in being interviewed or in her well-intentioned, although ill-conceived, offers of help. He is an example of the men who did not regain normal lives when they returned from the war. Kelly's father, also a Vietnam veteran, is a successful businessman, but he has consistently refused to discuss the war with his family. Kelly learns a lot about herself and her father as she finds out that interfering in other people's lives can have tragic results.

Fallen Angels
Written by Walter Dean Myers
Scholastic, Inc., 1988
309 pages

Richie Perry, a 17-year-old youth from Harlem, expresses his feelings and experiences throughout his year in Vietnam. The misery of his surroundings in a hot, humid climate infested with bugs and rats provides the setting for his hours of boredom interspersed with minutes of terror. He learns about dying and trying to keep himself and his buddies alive. Written as a narrative in the first person, the graphic language is typical for young men in adverse circumstances. The book is dedicated to Myers' brother, who died in Vietnam in 1968.

Little Brother
Written by Allan Baillie
Scotland: Blackie & Son, Ltd., 1985
Australia: Penguin Books, 1990
United States: Viking Penguin, 1992
144 pages

Eleven-year-old Vithy discovers talents and strengths within himself as he faces his fears and survives in the Cambodian jungles. Left to his own resources after he is separated from his older brother and surrounded by enemy soldiers, he figures out the direction he must travel to escape into Thailand. Once he reaches a border camp, he finds work and friends in the hospital, but his search for his brother seems hopeless.

My Name Is San Ho
Written by Jayne Pettit
Scholastic Hardcover, 1992
149 pages

In this first-person narrative, San Ho describes what it is like to be born into a world of war. Crops and all means of livelihood in his village, about 30 miles from Saigon, have been decimated. His father has died in the war, bombing raids have claimed the lives of many of his classmates, and his revered teacher is killed by the Viet Cong for teaching traditional history and literature. Fearing for his safety, his mother takes him by bicycle to Saigon. He lives in crowded conditions and attends school with other refugees for three years. Then he learns that his mother has married a U.S. Marine and has arranged for him to join them in Philadelphia. He is confused by this strange land where people speak a language he cannot understand and huge grocery stores have such an abundance of food. He is surprised that some people dislike him because of the color of his skin, but mostly he is overwhelmed with living in an environment free of war.

Park's Quest
Written by Katherine Paterson
E. P. Dutton, 1988
148 pages

Parkington Waddell Broughton V knows his father died in Vietnam when he was a baby, but he knows nothing else about him or his family. When he seeks out his roots by insisting on a visit with his grandfather, his findings are unexpected. His uncle has married a Vietnamese woman with a daughter close to Park's age. As he discovers Thanh's true identity, he comes to know himself and his deceased father better.

To Stand against the Wind
Written by Ann Nolan Clark
Viking Press, 1978
135 pages, bibliography

Eleven-year-old Em is overwhelmed with his sense of loss, both of family and tradition, as he begins to write about the past on the Traditional Day of the Ancestors. He thinks about his status as head of the household and the sad circumstances of losing most of his family during the war. He is concerned about Old Uncle and his sister, who are with him in this new land of America. This is a dramatic story of the destruction of Vietnamese family and culture during the war.

Sample Lesson Plan

Introduction

Read *The Wall* by Eve Bunting aloud to the class. Talk about the feelings expressed in the book. Think about each of the people mentioned and the reasons for visiting the Vietnam Veterans Memorial. How were their motivations the same? How different? Discuss what the students know about the Vietnam War, making a list of "facts" on chart paper to be used in a later session.

Building Background

Meet in the school library. Ask students to use books, computer programs, encyclopedias, and other reference materials to find significant dates concerning U.S. involvement in Vietnam. Have them work with a partner to construct a timeline showing these dates and the major decision makers. Appoint a committee of three or four students to use these timelines to construct a large timeline for display in the classroom during the remainder of the study.

Issues

Divide students into study groups to research and report on specific aspects and events of the war. These groups of three or four students should endeavor to become "experts" on their topics and prepare an interesting way of presenting information to the rest of the class. Possible topics include the French involvement in Vietnam, the Army of the Republic of Vietnam, the Viet Cong, guerrilla warfare, MIA's, The National Liberation Front, Operation Menu, the Tet Offensive, Vietnamization, conscientious objectors, antiwar movements, and the Vietnam Veterans Memorial. (Additional ideas for topics may be found in the following section of this lesson plan and in questions and activities included with this unit.)

Share information about topics researched. Refer to the list of "facts" generated by the students. Which ones proved true? Which were misconceptions? What questions still need answers?

Major Battles and Turning Points

Why did President Truman agree to send military aid to the Bao Dai regime in 1950? What resulted from the defeat of the French army at Dien Bien Phu? Why was the killing of two soldiers in Bien Hoa in 1959 significant? How did President Johnson's reaction to the Gulf of Tonkin incident escalate the war? How did the My Lai massacre affect public opinion in the United States? Why was the Tet Offensive a psychological victory for the Viet Cong?

Political and Military Leadership

Discuss biographies. The discussion can be based on some of the following questions. What is the difference between an authorized and an unauthorized biography? How are autobiographies similar to and different from biographies written by others? In what ways could autobiographies present a more biased viewpoint? Distribute a list of people who can be subjects of study for this unit. Possible people include: Ho Chi Minh, Dwight Eisenhower, Lyndon B. Johnson, John F. Kennedy, Richard Nixon, Ngo Dinh Diem, William Westmoreland, Nguyen Van Thieu, Nguyen Coa Ky, Vo Nguyen Giap, and Henry Kissinger. Assign students to groups of two to research each person and prepare a three- to five-minute interview with one student taking the part of the historical figure and the other serving as the interviewer.

Some students may choose to research and interview a representative of a category of people, such as a foot soldier, a noncommissioned officer, a doctor or nurse, a South Vietnamese peasant, a Viet Cong soldier, a refugee, a U.S. newspaper reporter, a television cameraman, a relative of a soldier who had been killed, a conscientious objector, or an antiwar demonstrator.

Projects—Preparing for a Videotape Production

Discuss the preparation of a videotape as a culminating activity. What responsibilities will the students have? How will the teacher and librarian support the students? What format will be used? How could graphics make the production more interesting? Should the art teacher be involved?

The basic content of the videotape can come from previous activities in this unit. Some of the best reports on issues and the best interviews can be adapted for taping. Consider including some dramatizations, such as a newly arrived soldier being told of conditions by those who had been in Vietnam for awhile or a conscientious objector being interviewed by military personnel.

Book reviews or round table discussions of books, especially fiction books with differing viewpoints, could add interest.

Fiction Books

Distribute a list of appropriate fiction books. Ask students to choose one book to read and prepare a critical analysis discussing literary qualities and insights acquired about the war. Multiple paperback copies of some of the most appropriate titles may be made available to students. (Using the reporting form for fiction books in Appendix B can help students to focus on literary qualities in their analyses.)

Divide students into groups or four or five, each student in each group having read a different book. Have small group discussions based on the students' written critical analyses. Then meet together as a large group to share insights.

Effects of the War

Read aloud *Angel Child, Dragon Child* by Michele Maria Surat or *Lee Anne: The Story of a Vietnamese-American Girl* by Tricia Brown. How were the lives of Vietnamese people changed forever by the war? Why did so many people leave their homes and become refugees? What have been the long-term effects on Vietnam?

How was the history of the United States affected? How were Vietnam veterans treated? Why was the Vietnam Veterans Memorial constructed?

Who attended the Paris Peace Talks? What were the terms of the agreement?

Culminating Activity

Complete the videotape about the war. A formal showing may be scheduled with invitations extended to parents, school and district administrators, and the public. If the tape is of high quality local cable or television stations might be willing to show excerpts as a public service. The tape can then be added to the school library collection.

Suggested Questions

How did the Gulf of Tonkin Resolution come about, and what was its significance?

Why was guerrilla warfare so effective against the U.S. forces?

In what ways did the conflicting beliefs of Buddhists and Roman Catholics contribute to the escalation of the war?

In what ways were China and the Soviet Union involved in the war?

More bombs were dropped on North Vietnam than had been dropped on Germany during all of World War II. How did the country continue to function?

How did the Tet Offensive prove to be both a military victory and a psychological defeat for the United States? Which results were most enduring?

How did the publication of the Pentagon Papers in 1971 influence public opinion about the war?

Why was the policy of Vietnamization a failure?

This has been called a living room war. How did the television coverage affect the war's outcome?

This has been called the Quicksand War. How does this metaphor apply?

Why was the draft necessary during the war? How did young men avoid being called up?

What types of alternative services were available to conscientious objectors?

Suggested Activities

Make a chart showing the numbers of U.S. troops in Vietnam and bordering countries from 1955 to 1973.

Prepare a dramatization of new soldiers arriving at a Vietnam base and being told about the situation by soldiers who have been there a while.

Make a chart showing the number of Amerasian children left in Vietnam as a result of the war. Indicate what has happened to these people as they have become adults and the influence this has had on the country.

Prepare a report or chart on present-day Vietnam. Include information about the long-term effects of the war on that country.

Interview Vietnamese people living in your area by telephone or in person. Report on their experiences in leaving Vietnam and on becoming established in the United States.

Glossary

accord—A diplomatic term for agreement.

Agent Orange—A chemical defoliant widely used in Vietnam that can cause cancer.

Agroville—An unsuccessful program sponsored by the South Vietnamese government to provide secure, fortified villages to prevent communists from disrupting the lives of South Vietnamese people.

ARVN—Army of the Republic of Vietnam (South Vietnam).

assassination—The planned murder of a prominent public figure.

black market—Illicit trade in goods or commodities in violation of official regulations; black markets often flourish during wartime.

body count—The number of soldiers and citizens killed during any given confrontation.

cold war—Rivalry between hostile nations that does not involve military conflict. The global rivalry between the United States and the Soviet Union that followed World War II was termed the Cold War.

communism—An economic system that places all land and other means of production and distribution under the control of the government.

Confucianism—A religion based on the teachings of the Chinese philosopher, Confucius (551–479 B.C.), which emphasizes harmony by subordination of individual needs for the good of the family, community, and nation.

conscientious objector—A person whose religious or philosophical beliefs do not allow him to engage in combat.

containment policy—The idea that communist expansion must be stopped and contained by Western powers.

counterinsurgency—A goal to undermine the influence of the Vietcong in South Vietnam through implementation of civil programs, including medical care, education, and agricultural aid.

defoliant—A chemical used to destroy jungles in Vietnam. Agent Orange was one of the most common.

demilitarized zone—An area that is prohibited from being used for military purposes.

democracy—Government based on the participation of citizens, either directly or through elected representatives.

détente—A relaxation of hostilities between the United States and the Soviet Union for a short time as they attempted to reach a position of peaceful coexistence.

domino theory—The basis for a commitment to the containment of communism, as compared to a row of dominoes set up; when the first one is knocked over, all of the others fall quickly.

dove—Symbolic bird of peace; denotes people who are opposed to war.

draft—A system for selecting young men to serve in the army.

draft dodger—A person who avoids the draft and does not go to war.

free fire zone—Area where anything moving would be shot down.

guerrilla—A civilian soldier who joins in surprise attacks on the enemy.

guerrilla warfare—A strategy of avoiding fixed battles, choosing instead to concentrate on ambushing patrols and sabotaging supply lines.

Gulf of Tonkin Resolution—Congress gave the president almost unlimited authority to use the armed forces to protect South Vietnam.

hawk—Symbolic bird of prey; denotes people who support military solutions to problems between countries.

insubordination—Refusing to follow orders given by a commanding officer.

MIA—Term used for soldiers missing in action.

Montagnards—Tribes in Vietnam's mountainous areas who fought with U.S. forces.

napalm—A jellylike substance, used in weapons, that causes prolonged burning.

National Liberation Front (NLF)—Governing body of the Vietcong established at the Communist Conference in Moscow in 1960 by Hanoi.

nationalist—A person who advocates independence for his or her country.

Operation Menu—Fourteen months of secret bombings, beginning in February 1969, against communist sanctuaries; approved by President Nixon but not revealed to Congress.

pacification—A program designed to win the support of people living in rural areas.

partition—The division of a country into separately governed parts.

Post-Vietnam Syndrome (PVS)—Emotional stress experienced by some soldiers as a result of their service in the Vietnam War.

POW—Term used for prisoners of war who were captured in battle.

search and destroy missions—The destruction of villages and areas considered dangerous to U.S. military forces.

shrapnel—A jagged piece of metal flying from an explosion of a grenade or other artillery shell; shrapnel caused many of the injuries to soldiers and civilians during the war.

Strategic Hamlet Program—The forced resettlement of rural farmers to fortified villages to protect them from the Vietcong and indoctrinate them in democratic policies.

Tet—The lunar new year as based on the Chinese and Vietnamese calendars.

Tet Offensive—A large-scale attack launched by the communists in January and February 1968 against the major cities in South Vietnam.

Tonkin—The northern area of Vietnam, dominated by the Red River Delta.

Vietcong—Nickname meaning Vietnamese communist; guerrilla forces fighting against the South Vietnamese and American forces.

Vietminh—Nickname for members of the Vietnam Doc Lap Dong Minh, the communist organization established by Ho Chi Minh in 1941.

Vietnamization—The withdrawal of American troops as military aid and assistance increased to the South Vietnamese army in an attempt to have the South Vietnamese take over more of the fighting.

War Powers Act—Passed in 1973, this act makes it illegal for a president to commit United States forces to overseas combat for more than 60 days without the approval of Congress.

Gulf War Literature Unit

Selected Chronology

1990	July 25	April C. Glaspie, U.S. Ambassador to Iraq, sent a cable to the State Department reporting on her meeting with Saddam Hussein. He had told her Iraq did not intend to invade Kuwait. Glaspie left for vacation a few days later.
	August 2	Iraq invaded Kuwait. The emir fled to Saudi Arabia. The U.S. carrier *Independence* was ordered to the Arabian Sea to support U.S. vessels in the Persian Gulf.
	August 3	Great Britain and France sent warships to the area.
	August 4	The European Economic Community (EEC) and Japan placed an embargo on Iraqi and Kuwaiti oil.
	August 6	The United Nations voted for worldwide economic and military sanctions against Iraq.
	August 7	The United States embarked on Operation Desert Shield with the stated purposes of defending Saudi Arabia and forcing Iraq to withdraw from Kuwait.
	August 8	American troops established positions in Saudi Arabia.
	August 10	Congress was informed of the U.S. troop deployment.
	August 11–12	British military personnel began arriving in Saudi Arabia.
	August 12	President Bush ordered a blockade of Iraq.
	August 13	Defense Secretary Dick Cheney went to the Persian Gulf.
	August 15	Saddam Hussein offered to make peace with Iran.
	August 18	Iraqi tankers proceeded into the Yemen harbor, but were restrained from unloading their cargo.
	August 19	Saddam Hussein offered to free all foreigners detained in Iraq and Kuwait, provided the United States would promise to withdraw its forces from Saudi Arabia and guarantee that the international embargo would be lifted.
	August 22	Nearly 50,000 U.S. reservists and National Guard troops are called up or placed on alert.

	September 10	The U.S. asked the European nations to send troops to the Persian Gulf.
	September 28	The U.N. Security Council voted to separate the questions concerning Kuwait and Palestine.
	October	Troop buildup from the U.S. and other countries continued to increase.
	October 16	President Bush was heckled by protesters in the first significant antiwar demonstration.
	October 23	General Colin Powell, the U.S. Chairman of the Joint Chiefs of Staff, visited the troops in Saudi Arabia.
	November	Troop buildup continued.
	November 4–5	U.S. Secretary of State James Baker visited the troops in Saudi Arabia and met with Saudi King Fahd.
	November 20	A U.N. resolution was passed endorsing limited military action if sanctions on Iraq had no effects by 15 January 1991.
	November 20	President Bush visited troops in Saudi Arabia.
1991	January 16	Allied forces began attacks on military targets in Iraq and Kuwait.
	January–February	U.S., British, and French forces secretly moved along Iraq's undefended border.
	February 22	Moscow announced that Saddam Hussein had accepted Soviet President Gorbachev's plan for withdrawal from Kuwait. President Bush proposed a counterplan that gave Iraq a week to leave Kuwait and included adherence to U.N. resolutions. Hussein did not reply.
	February 22–23	Iraqi soldiers blew up and set fire to more than 200 Kuwaiti oil wells.
	February 23	President Bush announced that he had directed General Schwarzkopf to use necessary force to eject the Iraqi army from Kuwait.
	February 23–24	Saudi troops and U.S. Marines drove through Iraqi lines to Kuwait in a diversionary maneuver. The XVII Corps set up fuel and supply stations in the desert. The 101st Airborne blocked retreating Iraqis.
	February 25–28	The threat of an amphibious marine assault kept Iraqi troops in Kuwait. Allied forces destroyed the Republican Guard and other Iraqi forces. U.S. Marines halted outside Kuwait City, allowing pan-Arab forces to formally reclaim the capital.
	February 27	General Schwarzkopf appeared before live cameras to explain the battle plan that had defeated the Iraqis in four days. President Bush announced a cessation of hostilities with a one-sided cease-fire that could be rescinded at any time.

March 3	General Schwarzkopf met with General Jabir al-Sabah of Kuwait, Lieutenant General Khalid bin-Sultan of Saudi Arabia, Lieutenant General Sir Peter de la Billiere of Great Britain, Lieutenant General Michel Rocquejeoffre of France, representatives of ten other coalition member companies, and eight Iraqi officers and two lieutenant generals to discuss arrangements for ceasing offensive military action.

Recommended Books

Picture Books

A Family in the Persian Gulf
(Families Around the World Series)
Written by Peter Otto Jacobsen and Preben Sejer Kristensen
Illustrated with color photographs
Bookwright Press, 1985
32 pages, glossary, index

The Al-Alrifi family of Bahrain, the smallest country in the Persian Gulf, is featured in this informative visit. Ahmed studied interior design in Cairo, Egypt, and works for the government in the Arts Ministry. His wife, Kawkab, works part-time in the Housing Ministry. They have two small children. The Muslim religion, traditional Arabic dress, and other regional customs are discussed.

Factual Books

Desert Shield: Fact Book
Written by Frank Chadwick
Game Designers' Workshop, Inc., 1991
64 pages, maps, chronology, bibliography

Presents a detailed summary of the preparations for the war, including descriptions and illustrations of weapons and war vehicles. The readiness of troops in all of the countries that would be potentially involved is charted and discussed. The book went to press in early January 1991, so it does not include the actual war.

Desert Shield: The Build-Up: The Complete Story
(The Power Series)
Written by Robert F. Dorr
Illustrated with black-and-white and color photographs
Motorbooks International, 1991
128 pages, chronology

Includes summaries of the military buildup in the Middle East by forces prepared to fight in the air and on sea and land. The feelings and experiences of specific people are mentioned throughout, providing a personalized sense of what it was like to be sent to a harsh desert climate to prepare for war.

Desert Storm: The Weapons of War

Written by Eliot Brenner and William Harwood and the Editors of United
Press International
Photographs (black and white) by Reuters International News Service
Orion Books, 1991 (paperback)
96 pages, maps

The Persian Gulf War was the first conflict in which high technology weapons were used. A brief history of Iraq's invasion of Kuwait and the military buildup is followed by four chapters describing personnel and materiel, the air war, the naval armada, and the ground warriors. Specific facts and details are included about all aspects of the war weapons used by both the United Nations forces and Iraq.

Iraq . . . in Pictures

(Visual Geography Series)
Prepared by Geography Department
Illustrated with black-and-white and color photographs
Lerner Publications Company, 1990
64 pages, maps, index

The geography of Iraq, its natural resources, and its cities are described. A summary of the history and government explains the years of wars and unrest in the area, especially the internal problems with the Kurdish minority and the Iran-Iraq War of the 1980s. The influence of Islamic religion and other customs provide insights into daily lives of the common people. A section on the economy and possibilities for the future conclude the book.

Middle East: A Background to the Conflicts

(Hot Spots Series)
Written by John Pimlott
Illustrated with black-and-white and color photographs
Gloucester Press, Franklin Watts 1991
36 pages, maps, chronology, glossary, index

The first three chapters provide a historic background of the conflict in the Middle East, the Arab-Israeli conflict, and the Iran-Iraq War. The fourth chapter is devoted to the Gulf War. Factfiles contain brief information about Middle Eastern countries and weapons used in the war.

The Middle East: The Lands and Their Peoples
(Silver Burdett Countries Series)
Written by Maureen Ali
Illustrated with black-and-white and color photographs
Silver Burdett Press, 1988
47 pages, maps, chronology, bibliography, index

Fifteen countries are grouped together and discussed in terms of their geography, religions, traditional lifestyles, economies, arts, foods, education, and leisure activities. A brief history beginning with ancient civilizations and continuing through modern-day politics is given. Historical conflicts, especially those concerning the establishment of Israel, are discussed. Statistics for each of the countries are included.

The Story of the Persian Gulf War
(Cornerstones of Freedom Series)
Written by Leila Merrell Foster
Illustrated with black-and-white and color photographs
Childrens Press, 1991
32 pages, maps, index

An exploring of some possible reasons for Iraq's invasion of Kuwait finds three main causes: oil, wealth, and ports. Following a discussion of each of these motives, a brief account of the war is given. The aftermath of the war for the nations involved, including loss of life, damage to land and cities, and ecological disasters, is described. The book concludes with some unanswered questions about the continuing unrest in Arab countries and the future of the United Nations in trying to maintain peace.

War and Peace in the Persian Gulf: What Teenagers Want to Know
(A Peterson's H.S. Special Report)
Written by Marian Salzman and Ann O'Reilly with Teresa Reisgies, Terry Barnett, and Several Hundred Teenage Contributors
Peterson's Guides, Inc., 1991 (paperback)
107 pages, chronology, bibliography

Using a question-and-answer format, this book was written while the war was in progress. Factual information is presented in the answers provided by the adults, while ethical and emotional concerns are revealed in the responses by young people. Issues such as the draft, conscientious objectors, and military service are addressed. Timelines of Persian Gulf history from 1932 to 1990 and from August 2, 1990 to January 15, 1991 document the continuing unrest in the area. Factual information about the countries of the Middle East is presented in a concise format. The book closes with a summary of the first week of the war.

War in the Persian Gulf
(Headliners Series)
Written by Fred Bratman
Illustrated with black-and-white and color photographs
Millbrook Press, 1991
64 pages, maps, chronology, index

Opening with the invasion of Kuwait, this book then moves into reactions around the world, including the outrage of other Arab nations. U.S. Secretary of State James Baker is quoted as having said that Iraq's control of Kuwait's vast oil fields placed the world economy in peril. Historical background about ancient civilizations in the area and the centuries of conflict are provided. Actions taken by the United States and the United Nations are presented and the actual conflict is summarized.

Biographies

Colin Powell
(Changing Our World Series)
Written by Jonathan Everston with Andrea Raab
Illustrated with black-and-white photographs
Bantam Skylark, 1991 (paperback)
96 pages, maps, chronology, index

Background information about the history and importance of the chairmanship of the Joint Chiefs of Staff opens the book. Powell's childhood experiences in Harlem and the Bronx and his ROTC (Reserve Officers Training Corps) training at the City College of New York are summarized. His distinguished service in Vietnam earned him a reputation for quick thinking, excellent command abilities, and bravery. His many honors and promotions and his role in designing the treaty between the U.S. and the Soviet Union to eliminate intermediate-range nuclear weapons are described. Soon after being chosen as chairman of the Joints Chief of Staff, he was called upon to deal with crises in Panama and the Philippines. The final chapter discusses his leadership in the military buildup and action of the Gulf War. Additional helpful information is provided in boxed text throughout the book.

Colin Powell: Four-Star General
(First Book Series)
Written by Elaine Landau
Illustrated with black-and-white and color photographs
Franklin Watts, 1991
64 pages, glossary, bibliography, index
Powell's childhood in Harlem and the Bronx are noted, as well as his distinguished record at the City College of New York, where he served in the ROTC. He demonstrated outstanding leadership qualities, receiving a Purple Heart in Vietnam. After earning a master's degree in business administration, he was selected as a White House Fellow. He served in command positions in Korea and at Fort Campbell, Kentucky. After graduating with honors from the National War College, he became a senior military assistant to the secretary of defense. President Reagan appointed Powell to the position of national security advisor and to the rank of four-star general. President Bush then chose him for chairman of the Joint Chiefs of Staff, a crucial position for shaping U.S. military action in the Gulf War.

George H.W. Bush: 41st President of the United States
(Presidents of the United States Series)
Written by Rebecca Stefoff
Illustrated with black-and-white photographs
Garrett Educational Corporation, 1990
122 pages, bibliography, index
This account of Bush's life opens with his distinguished military record in World War II as the youngest pilot in the U.S. Navy. He excelled at Yale University as both a scholar and athlete and became a successful businessman in the growing Texas oil industry. Although he lost his first bid for the Senate, he continued to work for the Republican Party and was elected to Congress in 1967. He later served as U.S. representative to the United Nations, chairman of the Republican National Committee, ambassador to China, director of the Central Intelligence Agency, and vice president

before becoming president in 1989. The first year of his presidency is briefly reviewed, including the aftermath of the Iran-Contra affair and Noriega's downfall in Panama. Bush is presented throughout as energetic and hard-working in all his endeavors.

H. Norman Schwarzkopf
(Changing Our World Series)
Written by E. J. Valentine
Illustrated with black-and-white photographs
Bantam Skylark, 1991 (paperback)
104 pages, maps, chronology, index

Schwarzkopf is introduced as one of the great American generals. As the only son of an Army colonel he was destined to go to West Point. Some of his childhood was spent in Iran when his father was stationed there. Schwarzkopf served two tours of duty in Vietnam, earning three Silver Stars and two Purple Hearts. He returned to West Point as an associate professor and worked his way through the ranks with various duties in the Pentagon interspersed with commands in Alaska, Washington, Hawaii, and West Germany. Throughout this process he earned a reputation for his devotion to keeping soldiers physically and mentally fit. In 1988 he was awarded his fourth star and appointed commander-in-chief of the U.S. Central Command. After the invasion of Kuwait, he presented a plan for a massive military buildup to President Bush and his advisors. This became the basis for Operation Desert Storm. He then led his staff in Saudi Arabia in planning and implementing the attack on Iraq. His military tactics and his leadership throughout the conflict are praised.

Saddam Hussein and the Crisis in the Gulf
Written by Judith Miller and Laurie Mylroie
Time Books, 1990 (paperback)
268 pages, maps, chronology, bibliography

This book is basically a history of Iraq with some mention of Hussein's rise to authority and his role in the country's affairs. The country is described as a bastion of fear and intimidation due to Hussein's inhuman treatment of political rivals and his use of terrorism as a legitimate means of foreign policy. The concluding chapter summarizes the authors' perceptions of the reasons for U.S. involvement in the Persian Gulf. The tone is somewhat critical of

President Bush and his advisors, emphasizing U.S. dependence on Middle East oil as the major reason for troops being deployed to the area. The book was published before the conclusion of the war, so outcomes are not discussed.

Schwarzkopf: The Man, the Mission, the Triumph
Written by Richard Pyle
Insert of black-and-white photographs
Signet, 1991 (paperback)
270 pages

The first half of the book presents a traditional biography of Schwarzkopf, beginning with some interesting background about his father and including the fact that Schwarzkopf spent part of his childhood in the Middle East. An extremely intelligent man, he attended West Point and, after earning a master's degree in engineering, returned to teach there. He earned three Silver Stars and two Purple Hearts during two tours of duty in Vietnam. In 1983 he was with the forces that invaded Grenada. He was in charge of the Central Command, which includes most of the Persian Gulf countries, when Iraq invaded Kuwait. Both his military and his diplomatic skills were needed for developing a battle plan, working with military leaders of Allied nations, and dealing with press corps from around the world. The second half of the book is composed of transcripts of an interview in September 1990, CentCom briefings in January and February 1991, and his address to departing troops on 8 March 1991.

Stormin' Norman: An American Hero
Written by Jack Anderson and Dale Van Atta
Insert of black-and-white photographs
Zerba Books, 1991 (paperback)
190 pages

This book begins with a brief biographical sketch of Schwarzkopf's childhood and early years. The major portion of the book describes the military buildup for the war and the actual conflict, featuring Schwarzkopf's role throughout.

Fiction Books

Only one fiction book about the war was located. Picture books and fiction books about wars traditionally appear later than factual books and biographies. Hopefully some good titles will be appearing soon.

The War Began at Supper: Letters to Miss Loria
Written by Patricia Reilly Giff
Illustrated by Betsy Lewin
Dell Publishing, 1991 (paperback)
69 pages

Beginning on 2 January and continuing through 18 February 1991, five children reveal their fears and anxieties about the war in letters to a former student teacher. Michael's father is in the reserves and is called up. Karl worries about terrorists bombing the school bus and begins walking to school. Private Helen Denning becomes Alice's pen pal, and Alice shares her letters. The students gradually turn to each other and form a type of support group for themselves. This book is appropriate for elementary school students and reluctant readers. Passages could be read to older students, and the format could spark some related activities.

Sample Lesson Plan

Introduction

Locate the Middle East on a world map. Point out Kuwait, Iraq, Saudi Arabia, the Persian Gulf, and other areas related to the Gulf War. Distribute outline maps of the Middle East to students and ask them to label the countries and bodies of water being discussed. Read *A Family in the Persian Gulf* by Jacobsen and Kristensen. Talk about the cultures of these countries and ways cultural differences can affect communication and understanding among countries.

Background Information

Present a historical look at the Middle East that includes the significance of the area for ancient trade routes, the influence of the Ottoman Empire, the arbitrary division of the area into countries at the end of World War I, and the importance of oil on the region and on the world economy.

Begin research to discover the causes of the Gulf War. The best sources of information may be past issues of news magazines and newspapers. Some CD-ROM programs specifically about the war are available and CD-ROM encyclopedias generally have updated information. Students may need to extend searches beyond the school library to public and university libraries.

Issues

Discuss the probable reasons for Iraq's invasion of Kuwait. How did Saddam Hussein justify his actions? Refer to the map of the Middle East again. Which countries belong to OPEC (Organization of Petroleum Exporting Countries)? How had OPEC attempted to pacify Saddam Hussein in the past? How would having access to the ports in Kuwait benefit Iraq? What countries depend on oil from the Middle East? Why was Kuwait unable to defend itself? How did the United States declare war on Iraq? How was the United Nations involved?

Major Battles and Turning Points

How was Saddam Hussein's announcement of the annexation of Kuwait received in the United Nations? What was the purpose of the economic sanctions passed by the U.N. against Iraq? How effective were they? When did Operation Desert Shield become Operation Desert Storm?

Political and Military Leadership

How had Saddam Hussein risen to power in Iraq? How did President Bush respond to Iraq's invasion of Kuwait? In what ways were Colin Powell and H. Norman Schwarzkopf well qualified to direct military action during the conflict?

Projects—Producing a News Magazine

Meet in the school library or visit a public library to look at back issues of *Time, Newsweek, U.S. World and News Report,* and other appropriate periodicals. What types of articles did they carry about the war? Have the class plan their own news magazine. How could a special issue, devoted entirely to the war, be organized? What topics and people should be covered in the articles? Would editorials expressing differing opinions be appropriate? Consider including original political cartoons.

Some students could contact local veterans of the war and interview them either in person or by telephone. Information from the interviews could then be written in a column format. Another column could feature information gathered from interviews with relatives of the veterans.

Effects of the War

How were the countries of Kuwait and Iraq changed as a result of the war? How did Saddam Hussein accept his defeat? Did the war end his threats of aggression in the Middle East? What happened to minority groups, such as the Shiites and Kurds, in Iraq? What are likely to be some of the long-term environmental consequences? What changes were made in the Kuwaiti government? How was Israel affected? What about other Middle Eastern countries? How did the role of the United Nations change? How was the response to returning U.S. veterans from the Gulf War different from the response to returning Vietnam veterans?

Culminating Activity

Publish the special issue of a news magazine. Distribute copies to students, parents, school and district administrators, and local news media. Don't forget to place a copy in the school library.

Suggested Questions

How are sanctions used to avoid war?

What sanctions were placed on Iraq after the invasion of Kuwait?

How effective were these sanctions?

Could more or different sanctions have been more effective?

What is the significance of the differences in the economies of Kuwait and Iraq?

What are the sources of conflict in Kuwait and Iraq over the Rumalia Oil Field?

How did the Palestinian problem affect the war?

How might the war have progressed differently if Israel had retaliated when Iraq attacked?

Why were tanks particularly important to the United States battle plan?

Which countries other than the United States sent troops to join in the conflict?

What role did the Soviet Union play in the conflict?

How did superior air power aid the United States in achieving victory?

Why was sea power important?

What could have been the consequences of Saddam Hussein's threats to use chemical and biological warfare?

What are the similarities and differences among the regular army, the U.S. Army Reserve, and the National Guard?

In what ways was the composition of the military personnel different for this war than for any other war in U.S. history?

What was the significance of yellow ribbons placed on office doors, on residence doors, in state legislator's chairs, and around trees?

What role did the United Nations play throughout the conflict?

Why did military leaders impose restrictions on the media in reporting about the war?

How could a country win a war and suffer from economic devastation as a result?

Why did President Bush decide to declare victory and stop the war before Saddam Hussein was eliminated?

Why did President Bush refer to the Vietnam War when discussing the victory in the Gulf War?

Why has the Gulf War been called the 100 Hour War?

What reparations were levied against Iraq?

In what ways can reparations against a defeated country be counterproductive?

How could the results of the Gulf War promote a movement toward worldwide disarmament?

Suggested Activities

Show the ancient trade routes on a map of the Middle East and explain why this area has often been plagued with conflict.

Research and report on the treatment of Kuwaiti citizens following the Iraqi invasion.

Design a chart showing the changes in governments and control in Iraq and/or Kuwait from the defeat of the Ottoman Empire at the close of World War I through the present.

Construct a graph showing the number of troops from each of the countries involved in the war.

Research and report on the similarities and differences in the media reporting of the Gulf War and the Vietnam War.

Design a chart illustrating the ecological effects of the war on the Middle East.

List the eight principles of warfare and explain how General Schwartzkopf complied with them in his war plan.

List Saddam Hussein's major mistakes in strategy. How could different decisions have caused different outcomes?

Soldiers stationed in Saudi Arabia reported that boredom was a major problem. Make a list of activities that could be enjoyed in a desert climate.

Create a board game or card game that soldiers could play in their tents or barracks.

Research and report on the threat of biological warfare.

Create a picture book illustrating the cultural differences in the role of women in the United States and Saudi Arabia.

Create a picture book illustrating displays of patriotism during the war.

Make a graph showing the amount of oil the United States has imported from Iraq and Kuwait from 1980 to the present.

Make a graph comparing the numbers of volunteers, draftees, minorities, and women in the Gulf War and the Vietnam War.

Develop a chart showing the ways military equipment was adapted for harsh conditions due to sand and heat.

Dramatize the experience of a man or woman in the military reserves being called for active duty, including them telling their families and employers.

Glossary

BPI (Ba'ath Socialist party of Iraq)—The political party of Saddam Hussein.

combat helicopters—Helicopters equipped with armament.

Desert Shield—The planning of a military response to Iraq's invasion of Kuwait.

Desert Storm—The military action against Iraq.

FASCAM (field artillery scatterable mines)—A system capable of laying antitank and antipersonnel mine fields quickly to protect moving mechanized forces.

friendly fire—Military action in which people are accidentally killed or injured by their own troops' munitions fire.

hostages—Individuals held against their will; foreign citizens caught in Kuwait at the time of the invasion who were not allowed to leave and were sometimes used as human shields by Iraqi soldiers.

ICM (improved conventional munitions)—Weapons capable of holding dozens of 40mm shaped charge grenades.

Kurds—A minority ethnic group in Iraq.

leapfrog—A strategy to supply Allied troops as they moved into enemy territory. Supplies would advance to the head of the line each time a new base was established.

MANPADS (man-portable air defense systems)—Shoulder-fired surface-to-air missiles.

NBC garb—Clothing designed to protect soldiers from nuclear, biological, and chemical warfare.

NVG (night vision goggles)—Goggles equipped with infrared sensors to visually transform night into day.

OPEC (Organization of Petroleum Exporting Countries)—A coalition formed to control prices and impose limits on the annual production of oil.

paratroopers—Military personnel who parachute into or near enemy territory.

Patriot missile—Missile programmed to hit any SCUD whose trajectory took it toward a worthwhile target.

SAM—A surface-to-air missile launched from a fixed mount or vehicle chassis to stop attacking aircraft.

SCUD missiles—A NATO code name for the Soviet SS-10 surface-to-surface missiles that were modified by the Iraqis to hit at ranges of up to 400 miles.

sortie—A single flight by an aircraft.

stealth technology—Military methods that allow enemy devices, such as aircraft or missiles, to slip through air defenses undetected.

tank—A tracked, heavily-armored vehicle whose main purpose is to carry a heavy direct-fire cannon.

thermal sights—Sights that use the heat generated by a target to detect it, even in total darkness.

Zulu—Designation for the standard Greenwich Mean Time (GMT) zone.

Appendix A: Planning Guides

Planning Guide

Thematic Unit:

Teacher(s):

Librarian:

Date:

What are our objectives for this unit?

What will be the student outcomes as a result of this unit?

Which students will be involved?
    Entire class?
    More than one class?
    Special interest group?

What skills will be needed for students to accomplish these objectives and outcomes?

How can the teaching of these skills be integrated into the unit?

Which skills will be taught in the school library?

Which skills will be taught in the classroom?

What resources do we need to reach our objectives?

Which of these resources are available in the school library?

Which of these resources are available in the classroom?

How will we acquire resources we do not have?
    Borrow from other classrooms in our school?
    Borrow from another school in our district?
    Borrow from a public library?
    Place an order for addition to the library collection?
    Place an order for addition to the classroom collection?

How many class sessions are anticipated?

Planning Guide cont.

Dates and times of class sessions:

What will we do each day?

How will we introduce the unit?

Will students meet in the classroom or library?
    Whole class?
    Some students in each place?

What supplies and resources will students need?

What is the teacher's responsibility?

What is the librarian's responsibility?

What will students be doing?
    Whole group activities?
    Small group activities?
    Individual activities?

What will we do for a culminating activity?

How will students be evaluated?

How will the unit be evaluated?

Planning Guide for Special Interest Groups

1. Identify students for participation.
   A group of six to ten students is usually best.
   Determine the general range of the students' reading levels.

2. Select a theme.
   Consider the interests of the students.
   Consider the potential for high levels of thinking.
   Consider the availability of books and materials.

3. Locate appropriate materials.
   Use the school library media center.
   Use the district professional library.
   Use the public library.
   Consider requesting loans from other school libraries.

4. Read books and preview audiovisual materials.
   Think about possible groupings.
   Think about required readings.

5. Organize the unit.
   Include a variety of types of books.
   Include books appropriate for students' reading abilities.
   Determine the requirements for readings and/or projects.
   Establish a timeline for group meetings and discussions.

6. Develop reporting forms.
   Include possibilities for a variety of thinking levels in the responses.

7. Initial meeting with students.
   Distribute copies of requirements for the unit and
      recommended bibliographies.
         Discuss the theme.
         Discuss the timeline.
         Establish guidelines for grading.
   Distribute copies of reporting forms.
         Read an appropriate picture book.
         Fill out a reporting form together.

Planning Guide for Special Interest Groups cont.

8. Subsequent meetings.
    Meet within two or three days to be sure everyone
       understands the reporting form and is progressing
       appropriately.
    Meet to read and discuss picture books.
    Meet to discuss books from each category: factual books,
       biographies, fiction books.

9. Evaluation.
    Grades may be based on the number of books read or the
       number of pages read, if reporting forms have been filled
       out correctly and participation in discussions has been of
       high quality.
    Ask students to write a summary of their reactions to the
       unit, including things they would continue and things
       they would change.

10. Revise the unit each time it is taught.
    Add new books.
    Delete ineffective books.
    Incorporate changes suggested by students when
       appropriate.

Appendix B:
Reporting, Recording, and Evaluation Forms

Reporting Form: Factual Books

Name _____ Date _____

Title of book _____

Author _____

Copyright date _____ Number of pages _____

_____

What qualifications does the author possess for writing a book about the war?

Did this book provide an overview of the war or focus on a specific event or aspect?

If it provides an overview, describe the tone of the book. If it focuses on a specific event, describe the significance of this event in the war.

What was the most important thing you learned about the war from this book?

Did the format of the book, illustrations, or photographs contribute to your understanding of the war?
Explain why or why not.

Would you recommend this book to your classmates?
Explain why or why not?

Reporting Form: Biographies

Name _____ Date _____

Title of book _____

Author _____

Name of person the book is about _____

Copyright date _____ Number of pages _____

This person is/was a citizen of what country?

Where do the events of the book take place?

What are/were the person's strengths?

What are/were the person's weaknesses?

How do the person's strengths and weaknesses contribute to the events of the story?

How is factual information about the war presented?

What is the most significant thing you learned from reading this book?

Reporting Form: Fiction Books

Name _____ Date _____

Title of book _____

Author _____

Copyright date _____ Number of pages _____

Where does this story take place?

How does the setting contribute to the meaning of the story?

During which year(s) did the story take place?

Describe the main character.

Did you care what happened to this person?
Explain why or why not.

What viewpoint does this story present?

Describe an important scene from the book.

Why was this incident important?

What was the book really about? Explain the theme of the book in one or two sentences.

Record Keeping Form

Students' Names	Factual Books	Biographies	Fiction Books	Number of Pages	Projects	Grade
1.						
2.						
3.						
4.						
5.						
6.						
7.						
8.						
9.						
10.						
11.						
12.						

Evaluation Form

Name_____ Date _____

Literature Unit_____

What I liked about this unit:

What I would change about this unit:

The best book I read during this unit:

I liked this book because:

I would like to be involved in another literature unit:

Yes _____ No _____ Explain why or why not.

Index

This Index contains titles and authors from the Recommended Books sections throughout the book.

---------------------------------**B**---------------------------------

C

─────────────────────**F**─────────────────────

─────────────────────**G**─────────────────────

--**H**--

---------------------------------------I---------------------------------------

---------------------------------------J---------------------------------------

---------------------------------------K---------------------------------------

L

M

N

O

—————————————————**S**—————————————————

T

—U—

—V—

———————————————Y———————————————

———————————————Z———————————————